FLYING HIGH

ISRAEL
FLYING HIGH

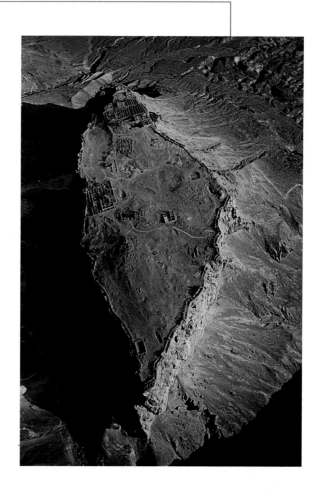

www.steimatzky.co.il

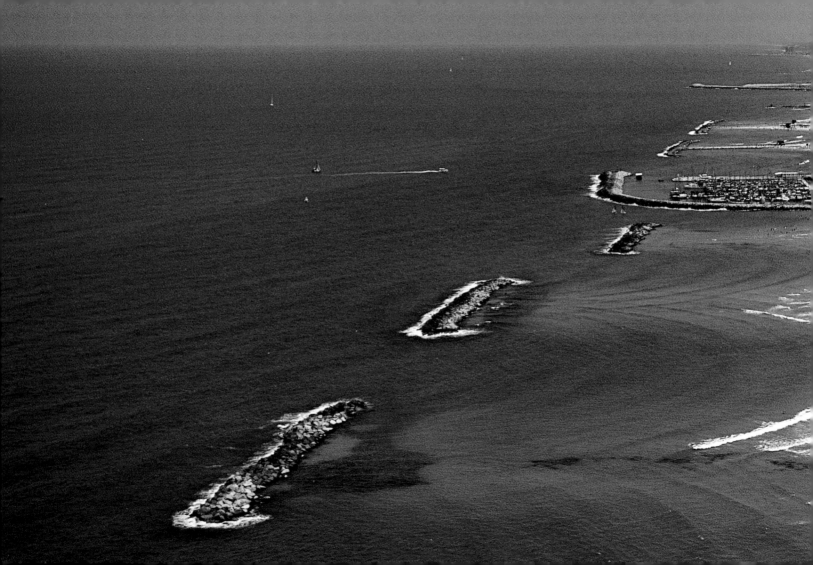

FLYING HIGH ISRAEL

PHOTOGRAPHS

Itamar Grinberg

TEXT

Hanit Armonn Grinberg

Editorial Director
VALERIA MANFERTO DE FABIANIS

Editorial Coordination
LAURA ACCOMAZZO
VALENTINA GIAMMARINARO

Graphic Design
PAOLA PIACCO

Cover
The Dome of the Rock sits in the center
of the Temple Esplanade, in the Old City
of Jerusalem.

Back cover
The fortress of Masada overlooks the Judean
desert from its 1312-ft (400-m) cliff-top location.

1
The flat summit of the Masada outcrop.

2-3
Jerusalem is sacred to the Jews, Christians and Muslims.

4-5
Hotels line the Tel-Aviv-Yafo conurbation,
the greatest in Israel.

Contents

6-7
Yavniel Valley is checkered with agricultural areas.

8
The Jordan River flows through a patchwork of irrigated plantations.

9
The Jaffa Gate opens in the western wall of Jerusalem's Old City.

10
A 623-ft (190-m) colonnaded way bisects the ancient city of Scythopolis.

11
The Golan Heights looking down on the north of the Sea of Galilee.

12-13
Rows of citrus plantation in the Beit Hakerem Valley.

14-15
The hotel area in Eilat with Aqaba and the Mountains of Edom.

FLYING HIGH ISRAEL

The
author

ITAMAR GRINBERG WAS BORN IN ISRAEL IN 1953. FOR OVER THREE DECADES HE HAS NURTURED HIS PASSION FOR PHOTOGRAPHY AS A MEANS OF DOCUMENTING CHANGE IN ISRAEL AND ELSEWHERE IN THE WORLD. DESPITE ITS RELATIVELY SMALL SIZE ISRAEL IS A COUNTRY WITH MANY NATURAL, SOCIAL AND POLITICAL FACETS, AND HAS FOLLOWED AN INCREASINGLY RAPID CONTINUUM OF METAMORPHOSIS THROUGHOUT THE SIX DECADES SINCE THE CREATION OF THE MODERN STATE OF ISRAEL. GRINBERG CAPTURES ALL OF THIS, LOVINGLY AND PRECISELY. GRINBERG'S WORK HAS APPEARED IN NUMEROUS PUBLICATIONS AROUND THE WORLD, AS WELL AS IN TELEVISION DOCUMENTARIES AND OTHER PRODUCTIONS. HIS OEUVRE CROSSES GENRE BORDERS, FROM THE DOCUMENTATION OF MANMADE CHANGES TO NATURAL TRANSFORMATIONS THROUGH TO THOUGHT-PROVOKING ADVERTISING MATERIAL. ABOVE ALL, HOWEVER, GRINBERG'S PRINCIPAL SOURCE OF INSPIRATION IS THE DYNAMIC EVOLUTION OF HIS NATIVE COUNTRY. HE HAS USED AERIAL PHOTOGRAPHY AS A PREFERRED MEANS OF CONVEYING TO THE OBSERVER NOT ONLY THE NATURAL BEAUTY ISRAEL HAS TO OFFER BUT ALSO THE FASCINATING HUMAN AND URBAN LANDSCAPES AS THEY UNCEASINGLY DEVELOP AND UNFOLD. GRINBERG HAS PUBLISHED SEVERAL BOOKS ABOUT VARIOUS ASPECTS OF LIFE IN ISRAEL INCLUDING *RITUALS IN JERUSALEM*, ABOUT THE THREE MAJOR MONOTHEISTIC RELIGIONS IN JERUSALEM, AND *ISRAEL FROM THE AIR*.

FLYING HIGH ISRAEL

Introduction

"ERETZ ISRAEL (THE LAND OF ISRAEL) WAS THE BIRTHPLACE OF THE JEWISH PEOPLE. HERE THEIR SPIRITUAL, RELIGIOUS AND POLITICAL IDENTITY WAS SHAPED. HERE THEY FIRST ATTAINED STATEHOOD, CREATED CULTURAL VALUES OF NATIONAL AND UNIVERSAL SIGNIFICANCE AND GAVE TO THE WORLD THE ETERNAL BOOK OF BOOKS.

"AFTER BEING FORCIBLY EXILED FROM THEIR LAND, THE PEOPLE KEPT FAITH WITH IT THROUGHOUT THEIR DIASPORA AND NEVER CEASED TO PRAY AND HOPE FOR THEIR RETURN TO IT AND FOR THE RESTORATION IN IT OF THEIR POLITICAL FREEDOM." [FROM THE DECLARATION OF INDEPENDENCE OF THE STATE OF ISRAEL]

ON MAY 14, 1948 (IYAR 5, 5708 ACCORDING TO THE HEBREW CALENDAR) DAVID BEN-GURION DECLARED THE CREATION OF A NEW STATE IN ERETZ ISRAEL, THE

18
The pastoral-looking church on the Mount of Beatitudes overlooks the Sea of Galilee where Jesus gave the Sermon on the Mount.

28
The aqueduct that served the city of Caesarea. At first, water was supplied from cisterns. Later, as the city grew, Herod ordered a supply system using external water sources to be built. The Roman emperor Hadrian upgraded it.

Introduction

STATE OF ISRAEL. THE DECLARATION CEREMONY TOOK PLACE IN THE OLD MUSEUM BUILDING ON ROTHSCHILD BOULEVARD IN TEL AVIV.

IT WAS A FRIDAY, SABBATH EVE, WHEN EVERYONE CROWDED ROUND THEIR RADIO SETS LISTENING TO THE VOICE OF DAVID BEN-GURION ANNOUNCING THE ESTABLISHMENT OF THE STATE. THOSE WHO HEARD THE BROADCAST WILL NEVER FORGET THE EXCITEMENT, THE QUICKENING OF THEIR HEARTBEAT, AND THE REALIZATION OF A DREAM. BUT, AT THE SAME TIME, A HEAVY AND FOREBODING SHADOW EMERGED AND THERE WAS A PALPABLE SENSE OF THE IMPENDING THREAT OF THE NEIGHBORING ARAB COUNTRIES' RESPONSE.

THERE WAS A FESTIVE AIR AND THOUSANDS THRONGED THE SYNAGOGUES AND OFFERED UP A PRAYER FOR THE WELL-BEING OF THE NEW STATE WHILE OTHERS SIMPLY BROKE OUT IN DANCE ON THE STREETS.

BUT THE RESPONSE, NATURALLY, WAS SWIFT. THE VERY NEXT DAY THE ARAB ARMIES INVADED THE NEW COUNTRY. THE WAR OF INDEPENDENCE BROKE OUT AND THE DAY-OLD STATE WAS ATTACKED. IN EARLY JANUARY 1949, WHEN THE WAR WAS OVER, THE GATES OF ISRAEL WERE THROWN OPEN TO ANY JEW WHO

Introduction

WISHED TO LIVE THERE. IN JULY 1950 THE LAW OF RETURN WAS PASSED WHICH GRANTED THE RIGHT OF IMMIGRATION TO ISRAEL TO ALL JEWS.

IN ORDER TO GAIN A SENSE OF FLIGHT, AND AN AERIAL VIEW, I DECIDED TO JOIN ONE OF THE AIRBORNE PHOTOGRAPHIC FORAYS. THE QUIET OF THE MORNING, THE ONSET OF THE NEW DAY, THE CHIRPING OF THE AWAKENING BIRDS, THE SNAP OF THE SAFETY BELTS, THE ROAR OF THE ENGINE . . . UP AND UP WE GO, AND JUST A FEW SECONDS LATER WE ARE RISING HIGHER AND HIGHER THROUGH THE WISPY WHITE CLOUDS.

YOU HAVE TO COME TO TERMS WITH A DIFFERENT ANGLE ON THINGS. YOU COULD SAY THAT THE RULES ARE VERY DIFFERENT UP THERE. SILENCE ENVELOPES YOU, THERE ARE NO RED TRAFFIC LIGHTS, THERE IS NO LITTER ON THE SIDEWALK, THERE ARE NO TRAFFIC JAMS WITH HONKING HORNS, AND YOU JUST FLY FAR AWAY FROM THE HUBBUB OF THE MORNING, AS THE NEW DAY BEGINS.

WE SET OFF FOR THE SEA OF GALILEE, THE BLUE AND SO TEMPTING LAKE INVITES ME TO DIP MY FEET IN ITS COOL WATERS, EVEN JUST FOR A MINUTE, BEFORE FLYING ON. THE GREEK CHURCH AT KFAR NAHUM (CAPERNAUM), WITH ITS

Introduction

UNIQUE SHAPE, LOOKS LIKE SOMETHING FROM A FAIRYTALE, THE PILGRIMS ARE ALREADY TAKING RITUAL BATHS AND LOOK LIKE ELONGATED WHITE SHAPES IN THEIR SPECIAL ROBES. NEAR THE MOUNT OF BEATITUDES A NEW CHURCH STANDS, BUILT AFTER THE POPE'S VISIT IN 2000. ITS STRAIGHT LINES AND GREY COLOR STAND OUT BETWEEN THE GREEN HILLS AND FLOCKS OF SHEEP SCATTERED NEARBY. THE CHURCH AT TABGHA STANDS IN SILENT WITNESS TO THE MIRACLE OF THE LOAVES AND FISHES PERFORMED BY JESUS. THE PILOT BANKS TO THE RIGHT AND SUDDENLY AN EXHILARATING SIGHT COMES INTO VIEW: "THIS IS THE YAVNIEL VALLEY" THE PILOT EXPLAINS. MY BREATH WAS QUITE SIMPLY TAKEN AWAY BY THE BEAUTY OF THE VALLEY WITH ITS INFINITE SHADES OF GREEN, BROWN AND YELLOW, IN SQUARES, STRIPES AND ALL MANNER OF OTHER SHAPES. I FELT AS IF WE HAD JUST BURST OUT OF A PAINTING, JUST BEFORE THE PAINTER RAISES HIS BRUSH TO ADD THE ORANGE SUN AS IT RISES TO HERALD THE START OF A NEW DAY. WE PASSED OVER THE CRUSADER FORTRESS AT TZIPORI AND WE COULD IMAGINE, EVEN FROM AFAR, THE BEAUTIFUL MOSAIC OF "THE MONA LISA OF THE GALILEE."

Introduction

OVER THE SHARON REGION, FLYING ABOVE THE ORCHARDS, MY NOSTRILS FILLED WITH HEADY SCENT OF CITRUS-TREE BLOSSOM, AND I COULD TASTE THE BITTERSWEET FLAVOR OF ORANGE JUICE. NEAR ATLIT, FISHERMEN STOOD ON THE TINY ISLETS OFF THE COAST WAITING FOR A BITE. I COULD ALMOST STRETCH OUT MY HAND AND UNHOOK THE FISH OFF THEIR END OF THEIR ROD. . . . I COULD FEEL THE TINGLING SALT ON MY FINGERTIPS, AND I COULD SENSE THE WARM SAND CARESSING MY FEET AS I WALK ALONG THE SEASHORE. THE MEDITERRANEAN STRETCHED OUT BEFORE US, AND THE RISING SUN PLAYED WITH IT AS IF SCATTERING A MYRIAD TINY GLITTERING DIAMONDS WHICH MADE ME BLINK. THE MEDITERRANEAN SHORELINE CONTAINS THE REMAINS OF THOU-SANDS OF YEARS OF LIFE, SOME OF WHICH WE HAVE UNEARTHED AND OTHERS AWAIT OUR DISCOVERY.

IMBUED WITH THE SENSE OF FREEDOM OF THE SEA, THE SACRED CHRISTIAN PLACES AROUND THE SEA OF GALILEE AND THE VERDANT FIELDS, WE SPED ALONG THE ROUTE OF THE HIGHWAY THAT LEADS TO THE METROPOLIS OF TEL AVIV. THIS IS ISRAEL'S CULTURAL AND BUSINESS CENTER. THE PROXIMITY OF EVERY-

Introduction

WHERE FROM THE AIR IS SO DIFFERENT. THE SCENE CHANGES SO QUICKLY, THE TREES, THE FLOWERS, AND THE WATER, GIVE WAY TO SKYSCRAPERS, OFFICE BLOCKS, APARTMENT BUILDINGS, TRAFFIC LIGHTS AND STREET SIGNS ON EVERY CORNER, AND PEOPLE WHO LOOK LIKE TINY DOTS RUSHING AROUND FROM PLACE TO PLACE. WITH THE CROWDED NOISY ROADS, EVEN FROM THE AIR YOU CAN SENSE THE CHANGING PACE, THE TENSION AND THE ROAR OF THE CITY...

THE SCENE IS EVEN MORE DIFFERENT OVER JERUSALEM. YOU CAN FEEL THE HOLINESS, THE RESPECT EVERYONE HAS FOR THE CITY. IN 1948 JERUSALEM WAS DECLARED THE ETERNAL CAPITAL OF THE STATE OF ISRAEL. JERUSALEM WEL-COMES THE FAITHFUL INTO ITS JEWISH, CHRISTIAN AND MOSLEMS HOLY PLACES. THE OLD CITY SURROUNDED BY ITS STRIKING WALL – IT IS ONLY WITH OUR BIRD'S EYE VIEW THAT WE CAN APPRECIATE HOW JAM PACKED WE ALL ARE AT OUR HOLY SITES: THE WAILING WALL RIGHT NEXT TO THE TEMPLE MOUNT AND THE CHURCH OF THE HOLY SEPULCHER. EVERYTHING IS SO TIGHTLY PACKED INTO THOSE WALLS THAT THE OLD CITY LOOKS LIKE A BOARD GAME WITH THE DICE PILED UP ON IT.

Introduction

IT IS AS IF JERUSALEM HAS ITS OWN SUN THAT LIGHTS IT UP WITH THE CITY'S OWN UNIQUE COLORS. IT IS RESPLENDENT WITH ITS SPECIAL CHARACTERISTIC SHADES OF GOLD, AS IF IT REALLY DOES GLIMMER IN THE LIGHT OF SOME OTHER SUN! WE ALL HAVE A SPECIAL PLACE IN OUR HEART FOR JERUSALEM, BUT WE STILL HAVEN'T FOUND THE WAY FOR US ALL TO LIVE TOGETHER. IN HIS SONG *THE WAILING WALL*, YOSSI GAMZU WRITES: "THERE ARE PEOPLE WITH A HEART OF STONE, THERE ARE STONES WITH A HUMAN HEART." EVERYWHERE WE CAN SEE STONE BUILDINGS, IN THE WALL THAT RUNS AROUND THE OLD CITY, THE WAILING WALL, THE HOUSES BUILT OF SPECIAL JERUSALEM STONE, ON THE SIDEWALKS. IF ONLY THE STONES COULD TALK. . . .

IN THE EVENING, THE DEAD SEA IS BATHED IN HUES OF TURQUOISE AND PURPLE. ITS PASTEL COLORS ENHANCE ITS HEALING POWERS NOT ONLY TO CURE PHYSICAL AILMENTS BUT ALSO TO SOOTHE THE SOUL. THE QUIET OF THE "SEA OF DEATH" RESONATES INTO THE FAR DISTANCE. THE MUSHROOMS OF WHITE SALT SOAR UP OUT OF THE WATER AND THE BATHERS GIVE THEMSELVES TO THE WATERS WITH LIMBS STRETCHED OUT WIDE, AS THEY FLOAT MOTIONLESSLY ON THE SEA.

Introduction

THE LIGHT OF THE SUNSET COLORS MASADA IN SHADES OF RED, AS IF TO COM-MEMORATE ALL THE BATTLES THAT RAGED THERE. THE REMAINS OF THE IMPRES-SIVE FORTRESS RISE UP PROUDLY AND POWERFULLY, AND THEIR PRESENCE DE-CLARES THEIR INVINCIBILITY. IF ONLY IT WERE POSSIBLE TO FRAME THAT VIEW. . . .

FOR ME ISRAEL IS NOT JUST ANOTHER PLACE. IT IS MY HOME, THE PLACE I WAS BORN. IT IS THE PLACE TO WHICH MY GRANDPARENTS FLED FROM THE HORRORS OF ICY EUROPE. IT IS THE COUNTRY IN WHICH MY PARENTS MET AND MADE A HOME, THE HOME WHERE I WAS BORN TO THE SMELL OF THE SEA AND WATER MELONS IN THE SUMMER, AND THE SCENT OF THE CITRUS BLOSSOMS IN THE WINTER. IT IS A COUNTRY WHOSE INHABITANTS, DESPITE ALL THE HARDSHIPS, ARE WARM AND WELCOMING. IT IS A COUNTRY THAT KNOWS PAIN, AND WHERE BEREAVEMENT IS NO STRANGER TO ANYONE. HERE, SMALL CHILDREN DRESS UP AS SOLDIERS ON THE JEWISH HOLIDAY OF PURIM, AND WHEN THEY TURN 18 THEY JOIN UP AND SERVE THEIR COUNTRY. EVERY PICTURE AND PLACE TELL ME A STORY, AND INVOKE MEM-ORIES – CHILDHOOD TRIPS, MY FIRST VISIT TO THE SEA, CAMPING BY THE SEA OF GALILEE, ENCHANTING DIVES IN THE WATERS OF EILAT, MY FIRST HIKE WITH MY

Introduction

CHILDREN. THERE IS NO ADVENTURE BOOK, AS FANTASTIC AS IT MAY BE, THAT CAN RIVAL THE HISTORY OF THE LAND OF ISRAEL, FROM THE DISTANT PAST TO THE PRESENT DAY. THE LONGING OF THE JEWISH PEOPLE FOR A HOMELAND OF THEIR OWN, THROUGH THOUSANDS OF YEARS OF EXILE, AND EVERYTHING THEY ENDURED UNTIL THEY COULD ESTABLISH A HOME OF THEIR OWN. "ON THAT DAY THE LORD MADE A COVENANT WITH ABRAHAM, SAYING: TO YOUR SEED I WILL GIVE THIS LAND. . . ." (GENESIS, 15, 18). THE CHILDREN OF ISRAEL HAVE EXPERIENCED TRIBULATION, WAR AND NUMEROUS CONQUESTS IN THE BATTLE FOR A HOMELAND, A BATTLE THAT CONTINUES TO THIS DAY, SHIFTING BORDERS, OCCUPATION AND WITHDRAWAL.

THE LINES HAVE CHANGED OVER THE YEARS, AFTER WARS AND PEACE TREATIES, AFTER THE WAR OF INDEPENDENCE AND THE SIX-DAY WAR, AND THE PEACE TREATY WITH EGYPT, WHICH INCLUDED THE RETURN OF THE SINAI PENINSULA, WHICH SHRANK THE SIZE OF THE TERRITORY GOVERNED BY ISRAEL. IN 1994 A PEACE TREATY WAS SIGNED WITH JORDAN, IN 2006 ISRAEL DISENGAGED FROM THE GAZA STRIP.

FLYING HIGH ISRAEL

30-31
The ancient fortress of Masada on the summit of an isolated
rocky outcrop on the eastern fringes of the Judean desert,
overlooking the Dead Sea.

THE ARAB-ISRAELI CONFLICT OVERSHADOWS EVERYTHING, AND STILL THERE IS NO SOLUTION IN SIGHT. DESPITE THE CEASELESS INTERNAL WAR, GROWTH AND DEVELOPMENT HAVE NOT BEEN THWARTED IN ISRAEL. THE HORIZON HAS CHANGED OUT OF ALL RECOGNITION, FROM THE FIRST SETTLERS IN KIBBUTZ HOUSES AND TRANSIT CAMPS, TO CITIES AND THE SKYSCRAPERS OF TODAY. THE AIRPORTS, SEAPORTS, FACTORIES AND DEVELOPMENT ZONES, AND HIGH TECH, SOME OF THE WORLD'S MOST ADVANCED AGRICULTURAL METHODS, AND THE PRODUCE THAT FINDS ITS WAY ROUND THE WORLD. WHEN WE WERE UP THERE, AMONG THE CLOUDS, WE WERE PASSED BY A GROUP OF PURE WHITE DOVES. I WANTED TO HOPE IT WAS A SIGN OF THINGS TO COME.

32-33
Mount Eshet is a chalkstone hilly ridge along the southern Negev
plains with geological wrinkles which give it a unique appearance.

34-35
The snow-capped peak of Mount Hermon seen from a distance. This
is the highest mountain in Israel and is shared by Israel, Lebanon
and Syria. The ski resort operates when there is enough snow.

THE CITY OF GOD
Flying High

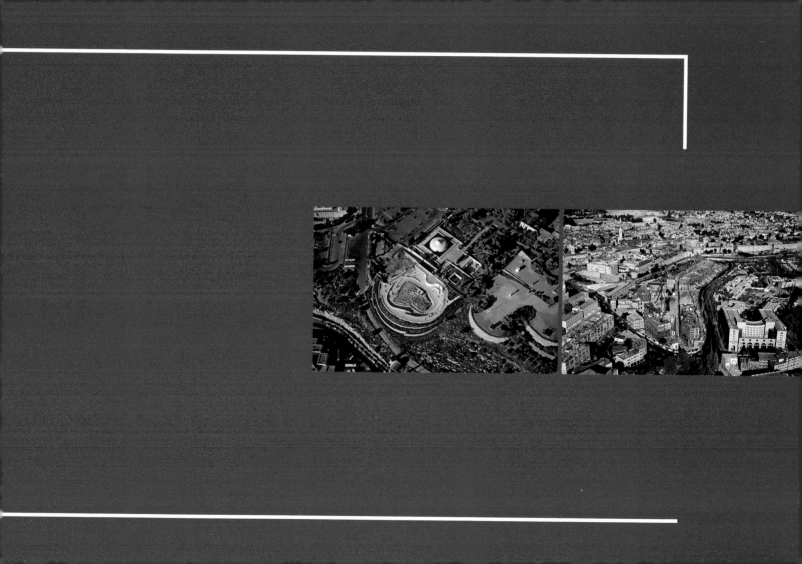

FLYING HIGH ISRAEL

37
The Shrine of the Book, part of the Israel Museum, has a distinctive dome and is surrounded by a pool (left). The David Citadel Hotel and the Mamila Compound lie opposite Jaffa Gate and David's Citadel in the Old City wall (right).

People swarm to Jerusalem from all over the world. People of all religions come to "immerse" themselves in it, in its spirituality, its holy places, its enchanting beauty and uniqueness. "For my house will be called a house of prayer for all the peoples. (Isaiah, 56, 7). You cannot help being moved by the sight of Jerusalem. It is simply irresistible. All your senses are heightened as you enter the city. You see sense in the background the sounds of Jews praying in synagogues, church bells peeling and a muezzin chanting from a mosque. The impossible actually exists. The fragile coexistence is real.

You wander between the city's buildings, built of Jerusalem stone. As you roam around the narrow alleyways you feel as if you are being drawn into a journey through time. If only the stones could talk, if they could describe the thousands of years of history, of wars, conquests and dispute.

On the streets, ultra-Orthodox Jews in traditional dress and beards and sidelocks mingle with nuns in black habits. Arab women with baskets on their heads, an Arab worker astride a mule, a Christian man of religion in his robe and a group of shaven-headed secular Jewish youngsters – a colorful human mosaic that is just a part of the charm of this fascinating city.

The sites that are holy to the three principal monotheistic religions stand side by side: The Western (or Wailing) Wall – considered to be the

38
Mamila, which used to be a residential area, now offers leisure and shopping facilities and a hotel; it is located near the Old City.

The City of God

holiest place in the world for Jews who come to pray by it, near the remains of the Temple. The plaza in front of the wall is divided into separate prayer areas for men and women, and there is a custom of placing slips of paper, with requests on them, in the cracks between the stones.

The Church of Holy Sepulcher – the spot where Jesus was crucified and buried, and which is considered to be the holiest and most important church; it is close to the Via Dolorosa where visitors can follow the route of Jesus' last journey, to his crucifixion.

The Dome of the Rock – which sits right in the middle of the Temple Mount –is believed to be the place from which the Prophet Muhammad ascended to Heaven. It is also considered to be one of the world's most beautiful and best known architectural works.

Toward the end of the week the special atmosphere heightens even more, and each religion busies itself with preparing for its special day – for the Moslems it is Friday, for the Jews it is Saturday, and the Christians it is Sunday. It is an exciting scene (even if seen from the distant perspective of an aeroplane window) – the preparations, processions, people wearing their best clothes and than all of them, each according to his or her religion, rushes off to their house of prayer and their ritual.

On December 5, 1949, about eighteen months after the establishment of the State of Israel, Prime Minister David Ben-Gurion declared Jerusalem the capital of Israel. "The State of Israel has and will have only one capital – the eternal city of Jerusalem, as it has been for 3000 years . . . We have declared and undertaken to history and the world that the State of Israel will guarantee freedom of religion, language, education and culture, will protect the holy sites of all the religions, and will be faithful to the principles of the charter of the United Nations."

His declaration was a natural continuation of

The City of God

the deeds of David who left Hebron and looked for a suitable location to build the Temple. He built the City of David in Jerusalem and his son Solomon continued his work and built the Temple on Mount Moriah (the Temple Mount). After Ben-Gurion's declaration of the capital of Israel, the government ministries were transferred to Givat Ram, west of the Old City. The Knesset (Israeli parliament), central government institutions, education and culture, the Israel Museum and Science Museum, and High Court are also located there.

At the end of the War of Independence, in 1949, Jerusalem was a divided city. The western part remained under Israeli control, while the eastern section was controlled by the Jordanians. The situation remained unchanged for nineteen years. In June 1967, when the Six-Day War broke out, IDF soldiers liberated the eastern part of the city from Jordanian control on the third day of the war. This act reunified the city.

The period from 1948 to 1967 was a difficult time for the Jews. In their hearts they longed for the Western Wall, but access to it was denied them. "The city that sits alone, and in its heart a wall" were the words the poet Naomi Shemer used to describe the city in her famous song "Jerusalem of Gold." Throughout these years the city was divided by a wall that ran between the Israeli and Jordanian halves. It was a Wednesday (the third day of the war), at 10 o'clock in the morning when the voice of Motta Gur, commander of the paratroop brigade, announced: "The Temple Mount is in our hands." There is no Israeli who does not quiver when he hears these words, and his eyes fills with tears at the sight of the paratroopers crying by the Western Wall on that day.

Jerusalem sits in the heart of the Judean Hills and is surrounded by hills of varying heights. The weather there is also special, as described in the words of the song: "Mountain air fresh as wine." A bird's-eye view shows the Temple Mount in the lowest spot in the city, with the hills around it and

The City of God

the special sites. Mount Scopus lies to the north-east of the Old City with the Hebrew University on its peak, and the Mormon University to the south. On the east – the Mount of Olives where one can look out over the old Jewish cemetery, and at one of the most beautiful churches in Jerusalem – Gethsemane ("All Nations"), with the Church of Mary Magdalene with its onion shaped golden domes, known as "the church of the onions." To the west – Mount Herzl with Israel's main military cemetery alongside plots for the nation's leaders, Zionist leaders and prime ministers, and where Prime Minister Yitzhak Rabin is buried. The top of the hill (which is named after him) is occupied by the grave of Benjamin Theodore Herzl, the founder of the State of Israel.

The Old City has been surrounded by a wall since the days of Ottoman rule. It was the son of Sultan Selim, Suleiman, who gave the order to construct walls around the Old City in place of the ruined walls dating to Crusader times. The wall is around 2.4 miles (4 km long) is 32.8 to 39.3 ft (10 m to 12 m) high and is between 13 and 16.4 ft (4 to 5 m) wide. A total of 24 watch-towers were built along the wall, the largest and best known being David's Tower. Eight gates were built into the wall – the New Gate, Damascus Gate, Herod's (Flowers) Gate, Zion Gate, the Dung Gate, Lions Gate, Jaffa Gate and the blocked off Golden (Mercy) Gate. Today the wall is used as a promenade and offers a view of the Old City. Jerusalem is one of the few cities in the world whose wall has remained intact, and has survived the city's growth over the years. From the air the wall appears to hug the city, gathering in and keeping the city's buildings together.

The Old City between the walls is divided into four quarters. The Jewish Quarter contains the most important site – the Western (or Wailing) Wall – in addition to the synagogues, one of the best known being the Horva. The synagogue has been destroyed and rebuilt several times (in Hebrew, "horva" means

The City of God

"ruins") and it was known as one of the most beautiful buildings in the city. After the Six-Day War the Israeli government had restored one of the four arches that supported the dome. The solitary structure became the symbol of the synagogue and of the entire area, but now the historic building has been completely reconstructed. The quarter also contains the Cardo, the remains of a section of the main thoroughfare of Jerusalem in Byzantine times. The Armenian Quarter is a religious, cultural and national center for Armenians in Israel and is owned by the Armenian Church. This is the smallest of the Old City quarters.

The Moslem Quarter includes the Temple Mount, Via Dolorosa, monasteries, mosques and schools for religious studies. This is the largest of the city's four quarters and is distinctive with its many mosques with their minarets.

The Christian Quarter has the Church of the Holy Sepulcher at its center. Nearby is the Muristan market area. The quarter contains over 40 holy Christian buildings which serve the various Christian sects.

Up to the 19th century all of Jerusalem was contained within the walls however, when the cramped conditions became unbearable and rents shot up, Jews started moving outside the walls and established new districts to the west of the Old City. The first quarter was built in 1860 – Mishkenot Sha'ananim.

The district was initiated and supported by Moses Montefiore (a Jewish philanthropist living in Britain), a windmill that was built then still stands there today. Other new neighborhoods sprang up – Nahalat Shivah, Meah She'arim, Mazkeret Moshe, Ohel Moshe and Yemin Moshe. The Arabs also established districts outside the walls, in the east of the city: Abu Tor, Katamon, Wadi El Joz and Musrara.

A bird's-eye view shows the central nucleus of the Old City, around which the modern bustling metropolis spread out with its tall buildings, industrial and high-tech areas, and a network of expressways around the city.

44-45

The city of Jerusalem nestles in the surrounding hills. This is a view of the Old City from the south. On the left is Mishkenot Sha'ananim, the first quarter to be built outside the Old City walls.

46-47

Ancient Jerusalem nestles between its walls, with the Judean Desert behind it.

FLYING HIGH ISRAEL

49

The New Gate is located near the northwest corner of the Old City wall. The gate's name stems from the fact that it is the most recent gate there, built in the city wall in 1889. The New Gate leads to the Christian Quarter. The Temple Mount and Mount of Olives can be seen in the distance.

50-51
Damascus Gate is considered to
be the most beautiful of all the Old
City's gates and leads to the city's
Muslim Quarter.

52-53
The Dormition Abbey is an impressive building with turrets and a bell tower.

54-55
The Church of the Holy Sepulcher in the center of the Old City's Christian Quarter is, according to Christian tradition, located on the site of the crucifixion and burial of Jesus. It is one of the most important and holiest churches in the Christian world.

56

56
Mercy Gate is located on the eastern side of the Old City. According
to Christian tradition it was through
this gate that Jesus entered
Jerusalem, and Christians call it
the Golden Gate.

57
The Christian Quarter is located in
the northwestern section of the
Old City.

FLYING HIGH ISRAEL

59
The Dome of the Rock, at the center of the Temple Mount, forms part of the Al Aqsa compound. The building is a beautiful Jerusalem architectural landmark that has become something of a symbol of the city. In 1994 the dome was renovated and recoated with 330 lbs (150 kg) of pure gold.

60
The Temple Mount, also known as Mount Moriah, is sacred to the world's three major monotheistic religions – Judaism, Islam and Christianity. The mount contains the Dome of the Rock, the Al Aqsa Mosque and the Western Wall.

61
The Al Aqsa Mosque is one of several Islamic religious structures located on the Temple Mount.

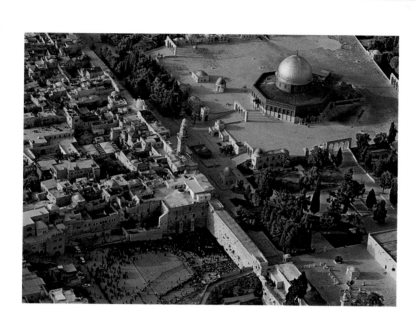

62
The Western Wall is the holiest spot on Earth for Jews. The piazza is divided into two sections, one for men and one for women, who pray separately.

63
The Temple Mount contains the juxtaposed Golden Dome and the Western Wall.

FLYING HIGH ISRAEL

65
The ancient Jewish cemetery on the Mount of Olives is overlooked by the Seven Arches Hotel.

66
The Russian Church and monastery are located on the Mount of Olives opposite the Old City Walls.

67 left

The Russian Church has a 210-ft (64-m) bell tower. The bell weighs at least 8 tons and was transported there manually from the port of Jaffa by pilgrims. It was the first bell to be rung in Jerusalem after several hundreds of years during which the city's Moslem authorities prohibited Christians from ringing bells

67 right

The Dominus Flevit Church on the slope of the Mount of Olives is designed in the shape of a tear and is also known as the Church of the Tear.

68

The Mount of Olives, with the old Jewish cemetery to the right, the Russian Church and Mary Magdalene in the center, and the Basilica of the Agony below.

69

Basilica of the Agony, also known as the Church of All Nations, is located at the foot of the Mount of Olives. The impressive building at the front has four pillars that support a mosaic with an image of Jesus. The roof has 12 domes, each with details of the nation it depicts.

70
A view of the Old City from Jaffa Road leading to Jaffa Gate, with the Russian Compound to the left of the road, with the Russian Church and new Municipality building.

71
Safra Square, built in 1993, serves as part of the Municipality of Jerusalem complex.

72

A view of the YMCA and King David Hotel, the Mishkenot Sha'ananim quarter, Sultan's Polls and Sacher Park to the left, the Old City nestling between its walls and the Mount of Olives to the west.

73

A view of the Old City from the northeastern corner, with the Rockefeller Museum outside the walls.

74
Route 1 leads from Jerusalem's northern quarters to the Old City. The Arab quarters lie to the left of the road, and the Jewish quarters to the right.

75 left
The Regency Hotel in Jerusalem is located at the foot of Mount Scopus.

75 right
The main entrance to Jerusalem.

76
The Jewish quarters of Beit Yisrael and Meah She'arim, with the Mount of Olives and the Judean Desert behind.

77
The Meah She'arim quarter and the striking circular Ethiopian Church.

78

In 1986 a competition was held for a design for the new Supreme Court building in Jerusalem, near the Knesset and the Government Quarter. The modern building was officially opened in November 1992, designed by the Carmi architectural firm and financed by the Rothschild Foundation.

79

The Israel Museum is located at Givat Ram. It is the largest and most important museum in Israel and houses collections of archeology, Judaica, Israeli art and exhibits from around the world.

80
The Valley of the Cross, named after the Church of the Cross, sits between the residential district of Rehavia, Sacher Park, the Knesset, the Government Quarter, the Givat Ram Stadium and the Israel Museum in Jerusalem.

81
The Knesset (Israeli parliament) is located near to the Government Quarter and Givat Ram in Jerusalem. The Knesset is the legislative body in Israel and comprises 120 members who serve four-year terms.

82

The Valley of the Cross contains a church and monastery from the Byzantine Era, one of the few to have survived in their entirety since that time. The monastery looks like a fortress surrounded by a stone wall. The site features a square bell tower and a silver dome on top of the church.

83

Yad Vashem is the world's largest Holocaust memorial and includes museums, monuments, statues, memorial stones, a memorial tent, etc.

84

The Hebrew University of Jerusalem is located on Mount Scopus, with the eastern quarters of the city in the background.

85 left

The Augusta Victoria compound sits at the top of the Mount of Olives and contains a church with a prominent bell tower, a hostel for pilgrims and a hospital.

85 right

Hadassah Hospital on Mount Scopus.

86

The Har HaMenuhot cemetery, 2460 ft (750 m) above sea level, is the main Jewish cemetery on the western side of Jerusalem. Mevasseret Zion can be seen in the distance.

87

The town of Mevasseret Zion sits, enveloped in morning mist, on a ridge in the Jerusalem Hills about 6.2 miles (10 km) west of the city.

88
The striking Notre Dame Church in Kiryat Ye'arim is located in the village of Abu Ghosh.

89

The Notre Dame Church at Kiryat Ye'arim, in Abu Ghosh, was built in 1918 on top of the remains of an earlier church from the Byzantine Era. There is a statue of Mary holding her son on the roof standing on the Ark of the Covenant, with angels on either side of her.

90

Church of the Visitation and the Gorny Convent are located in the picturesque rustic district of Jerusalem.

91

Shaar Hagai, with the highway from Tel Aviv to Jerusalem.

FLYING HIGH ISRAEL

93

The Israeli Armored Corps Museum and commemorative site is located near Latrun
Junction in the Ayalon Valley.

THE OCHER AND THE BLUE

FLYING HIGH

FLYING HIGH ISRAEL

95
The harbor of Akko, the ancient Acre, is mostly used today by
local fishermen and tourists (left). The rocks near the seashore
are a typical feature of Mediterranean beaches (right).

The Mediterranean Sea is Israel's western border; most of the country's other borders run alongside deserts. In fact, one could call the western border the country's "blue lung." The coastal plain that runs along the seafront stretches from Rosh HaNikra in the north to the Gaza Strip in the south; prior to 2005 the border stretched southward to Egypt but, after Israel's withdrawal from Gaza and its transfer to the Palestinians, Israel's Mediterranean border is significantly shorter.

In the ancient world the Mediterranean served as a main transportation route and as the basis for the growth of important and varied cultures that developed along its shores. Up to the 1920s the coastal strip was sparsely populated. Over the years and, particularly, since the establishment of the state of Israel, the coastal area has become heavily populated, with over 70 percent of the Israeli population now living there. Initially, agricultural settlements were established, based on local agriculture. One of the main areas of activity was the citrus fruit sector, with most of the crop designated for export. Even today, many orchards dot the coastal plain.

Built-up areas are now numerous along the coastal strip, and, from the air it is easy to distinguish the cities and townships from the agricultural settlements by the style of buildings, and how closely they are adjacent to each other. The first urban structures were comprised of low and spacious buildings but, as the cities evolved and land prices soared, tall building started appearing

96
The northern slopes of Mount Carmel meet the sea at Haifa,
near the harbor.

The Ocher and the Blue

that were more closely packed together. In the *moshavim* (villages) outside the towns, one can see single story houses with yards around them. Over the years there has been much construction along the seafront with marinas, harbors, jetties, breakwaters, piers, hotels and residential buildings going up. And, of course, Most of Israel's large towns have been built and have developed along the coast.

Past activity in the region left archaeological remains, both along the coast and in areas with shallow water. One of the best known sites is Caesarea where one can clearly see archaeological remains of the ancient harbor in the shallow water. Excavations there have uncovered wrecked ships, with their cargo intact, which offer us more glimpses of the past in this area.

The sheer white cliffs which mark the Israeli-Lebanese border, rise high above the sea. Their bright color stands out in stark contrast to the deep blue of the water below. The chalk rocks that cascade down to the sea are an outstanding natural phenomenon, and leave no room for beaches. An aerial view reveals the striking beauty of the region along with a glimpse of the fascinating local marine life in the caves below.

The northern coastal plain includes one of Israel's oldest port towns – Acre (Akko). A bird's eye view of the city shows the old quarter surrounded by a wall that was built in about 1800-1814 and which was designed to protect the city's residents. To this day there are several cannon stationed there, alongside three towers.

There is a large mosque inside the walls, and a hamam (old bath house), which were built at the end of the 18th century. There is also a fortress that was constructed during Turkish times, below which archaeological excavations revealed six

The Ocher and the Blue

knights' halls and the remains of an old Gothic church.

Today, Akko is a tourist center and offers a colorful market, archaeological sites, narrow alleyways, a promenade along the walls and beaches. The city also houses a world center of the Bahá'i faith, the followers of which regard Akko as a sacred place, and aerial photographs show the beauty of the carefully tended gardens of the Bahá'i temple there. In 2001 UNESCO designated Akko as a World Heritage Site.

Another and larger Bahá'i center can be found in the city of Haifa; it also serves as a world center for followers of the faith. The stepped gardens are spectacularly beautiful, and impressive in their colors and symmetrical forms: for a moment they even seem unreal. The gardens also contain several impressive buildings, and are in themselves a tourist attraction.

Haifa is Israel's third largest city, and is a center for the north of the country, and houses Israel's second largest harbor (Ashdod is the largest port). The port was first mentioned in the year 104 BCE, and the current harbor was opened in 1933 and provides a major source of livelihood for the city and the entire region. The vicinity also includes major oil refineries, factories and chemicals industries and related commercial and services facilities.

Haifa spreads out over a large part of the Carmel Hill, from the topmost ridges down to the lower plain. The city has an airport, train stations and is the only urban center in Israel with a subway (considered to be the smallest in the world). It also has institutes of higher education, including Haifa University, the medical faculty and the Technion. Haifa offers a wide range of leisure, culture and entertainment facilities and events, including

The Ocher and the Blue

arts, science and technology museums, and marine displays.

The city can be divided into two parts – the hilly area which contains most of the residential quarters, and the low-lying coastal strip with the bay, port and industry. Haifa occupies a unique location, from the heights of Mt Carmel down to the bay and the sea.

The Sharon region, the central coastal plain, includes the large, central and modern city of Tel Aviv. Tel Aviv has its own unique character, and bustles with a ceaseless fast pace of life. It offers a rich range of cultural, arts and leisure possibilities and has been dubbed "the city that never sleeps," an accurate description of life there. It is the first Jewish city, founded in 1909, and gradually grew among the sand dunes and beaches. Today, one can still see the red-roofed small houses of Naveh Tzedek, one of its first quarters.

Tel Aviv is a densely constructed city. In the last decade many skyscrapers have sprung up. One of the tallest buildings is the round tower of the Azrieli Center located near the Ayalon Freeway. The tower sits next to a busy junction and rises up to a height of 613 ft (187 m). The shortage of land and apartments in the city has pushed prices up and many people have moved out and now commute daily between home and work.

Tel Aviv is Israel's main financial and cultural center, and as such offers numerous employment opportunities. It contains the army's General Staff headquarters, a large number of embassies, mass-circulation newspapers, educational and cultural institutions, universities, museums, theaters etc.

Along the seafront there are lively hotels located next to each other, all with distinctive balconies that face the sea. The beaches are jam-

The Ocher and the Blue

packed on weekends and are a major leisure spot, particularly during the hot summer months. Watersports are also well developed and, like other Mediterranean cities, Tel Aviv has a busy marina and jetties. To the south of Tel Aviv lies the ancient picturesque port town of Jaffa.

In the past, Jaffa was an important port town owing to the advantages of its coastal position in a small natural bay sheltered from the winds. Before the ports at Haifa and Ashdod were established, Jaffa served as the gateway to the country, both for passengers and goods. Today, Jaffa attracts large numbers of visitors, both from Israel and abroad, who wander among its narrow alleyways that run between its art galleries, fish restaurants and the old port, which mainly services local fishermen. Jaffa also contains a mixed population of Jewish and Arabs who live side by side in the city. A view from above during the late afternoon hours, as the sun sets, shows the crowded houses and the winding shoreline of the small port basking in the gold of the sun, giving the appearance of a beautiful picture-postcard town.

On the southern coastal strip, just a few miles north of the Gaza Strip, lies the city of Ashkelon. It is one the world's oldest cities that has always served as a transit port town. Alongside the remains of the port and the ancient city, a new and modern city has sprung up with high-rise residential blocks. Ashkelon is one of the greenest cities in Israel, with its gardens and old orchards juxtaposed by the new gardens that have been cultivated in recent years.

The area between Ashkelon and the border offers beautiful white sand beaches with sparkling nature reserves that enable visitors to observe wildlife in an untouched open natural setting.

102-103
The ancient picturesque port town
of Jaffa. The harbor is still used by
local fishing boats.

104-105
The red roofs of the picturesque town of Jaffa on the Mediter-ranean coast. The coastline curves towards Tel Aviv.

106
Highrise hotels dot the mediterra-
nenan coast at Tel Aviv.

107
The promenade and beaches
along the Tel Aviv seafront to Jaffa.

108-109

Three skyscrapers – the round, square and triangular Azrieli Towers, the tallest of which is 613 ft (187 m) high – are located in the center of Tel Aviv, near the Ayalon Freeway.

110
The Ayalon Bridge and the towers of the diamond exchange and commercial center in Ramat Gan near Tel Aviv.

111
Tel Aviv – the three Azrieli towers – triangular, round and square. The Azrieli Center leisure and shopping mall is located between the towers.

112-113
The Tel Aviv skyline from the south.

114
Dizengoff Center on Dizengoff Street, one of Tel Aviv's main streets.

115 left
The Yarkon Cemetery in the central region of the country, near Petah Tikva.

115 right
The Center for Performing Arts in Tel Aviv.

116-117
Early evening, Tel Aviv bathed in the colors of the sunset, with the lights of buildings and cars in the distance.

118
The hotels along the coastal strip at Netanya. The coastline features high gravel outcrops.

119
Along the southern coastal strip – the city of Ashdod, a young and dynamic city which, over the years, has absorbed large numbers of immigrants. Ashdod contains Israel's largest port.

120
Naharya is located in the Western Galilee between Akko and the cliffs of
Rosh HaNikra, which can be seen in the distance.

121
Sunbathing at Gaash Beach, a stretch of golden sands a short distance
from Kibbutz Gaash and north of Tel Aviv.

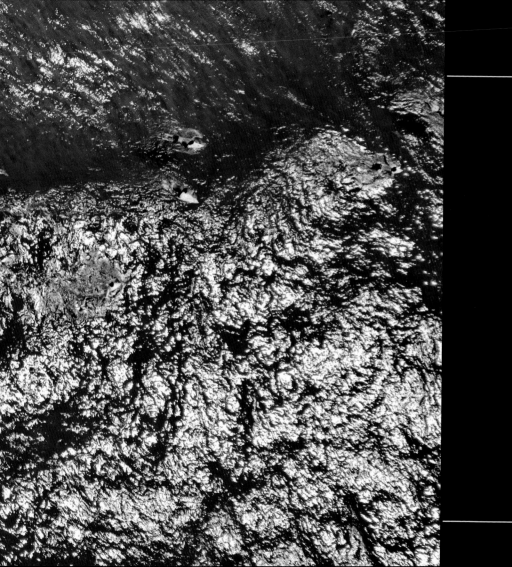

122-123
Water sports – such as windsurfing, wave surfing, jet skiing and sailing – are very well developed in the Mediterranean.

124

124
A speedboat and the sea – having fun is an easy task in the waters off Qesarya, the ancient Caesarea.

125
Group training of windsurfers in the Caesarea area.

126
Ramat Hanadiv is a large park south of Zikhron Yaakov. The park is built around the graves of Baron Rothschild and his wife. The gardens contain walking routes, archeological sites and an amphitheater where concerts are held in the summer.

127
The salt production pools between Atlit and Nevah Yam were built over the remains of ancient pools from Roman times.

128
Haifa spreads down the slopes of Mount Carmel to the Mediterranean
coastline.

129
Dan Carmel Hotel, Bahá'i Center and the wide boulevard that traverses
the Haifa's German Colony quarter.

130

Hotels on the ridge of Mount Carmel overlook Haifa, its bay and the sea.

131

The residential quarters along the ridge of Mount Carmel are surrounded by verdant growth and overlooking Haifa Bay below.

132
The Bahá'í Center is located in the center of Haifa and is a well-known
local landmark. The striking building in the center, with the golden dome,
is the burial place of the founder of the faith and is surrounded by neat
and spectacular gardens.

133
Haifa along the slopes of Mount Carmel, with the Bahá'í Centre sprawl-
ing across the center.

134

134-135

Akko, one of the world's most ancient port towns, is built on a sort of peninsula that juts out into the sea. The ancient city is surrounded by a wall that encompasses a large number of buildings from different eras, including a fortress, mosque, synagogues and churches.

136
The Western Galilee stretches along the Mediterranean coast, from Rosh Hankira at the northern end to the walls of ancient Akko.

137
The ancient port town of Akko juts out into the sea and is surrounded by a wall.

138
The Al-Jazzar Mosque – one of the most impressive and prominent buildings in Akko, built in the late 18th century.

139
Just outside Akko, the Mansion of Bahjí is surrounded by magnificent gardens open daily to the public. The Mansion was the residence of the persian prophet Bahá'u'lláh (1817-1892), founder of the syncretic Bahá'í Faith.

140 left
South of the Akhziv National Park, a beach stretches along the Mediterranean Sea.

140 right
Rich animal life thrives among the rocks of Akhziv Beach, above and below the surface.

141
The Akhziv National Park is situated on a rocky beach with lagoons, and natural and manmade sea pools.

142 and 143
Along the entire Mediterranean coastline, from north to south, there are miniature islets that comprise tiny nature reserves. They offer a habitat for water fowl, birds and a wide range of animal life.

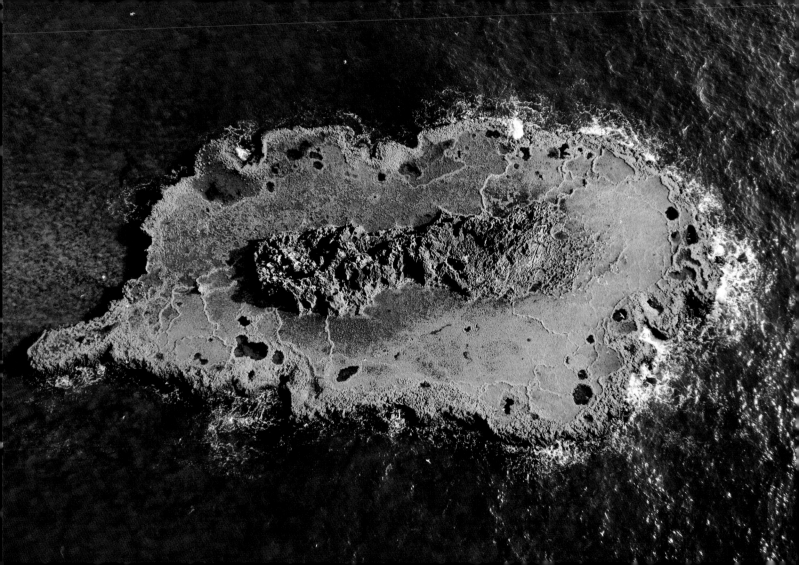

144
The Western Galilee with banana groves close to the coast near Akhziv.

145
The sheer white cliffs of Rosh HaNikra roll down to the blue waters of the
Mediterranean Sea.

THE DUST OF TIME

Flying High

FLYING HIGH ISRAEL

147
The Crusader castle of Monfort, in Upper Galilee, was the
headquarter of the Teutonic Kinghts (left). The Roman theater of
Scythopolis – Beit She'an – is one of the most impressive remains
found there. The theater had a seating capacity of 7000 (right).

No one living here today can ignore what preceded us. Our history is the basis of our existence. The present in which we live is a direct continuation of the past, of hundreds and thousands of years ago. It feels as if everything has happened here. This is a small country with a wealth of experience.

The geographical location of the Land of Israel, at one of the most important intercontinental crossroads of ancient times, drew great interest. Many peoples lived there with all manner of cultures, and war raged in it, almost incessantly, for many years. The special standing of the biblical land, and its association with the three main monotheistic religions – Judaism, Christianity and Islam – attracted large numbers of researchers looking to explore the country's rich past. Many researchers tried to identify the sites mentioned in the Scriptures.

At the beginning of the 19th century the remains and ruins of settlements were discovered and identified all over the country. In 1865 the British Palestine Exploration Fund was established and began conducting extensive surveys throughout the land, and all the ruins and sites its archaeologists discovered were recorded. In the 1890s professional archaeological excavations were begun at various sites, and these were supported by precise records of the actual work carried out and of the finds that were made.

148
The northern face of the Masada cliffs with the Northern Palace,
bathhouse, storage facilities and residential buildings located at the edge
of the top level. The surrounding wall can be seen. The summit of
Masada is a plateau that overlooks the Dead Sea.

The Dust of Time

In 1920 the government founded the Antiquities Department, and the Antiquities Law was drafted. Over the years hundreds of sites have been excavated, from Gamla in the north to the Nabatean city of Ovdat in the south.

In 1947, one of the most important archaeological finds the world has ever seen was announced – the Dead Sea Scrolls. They were discovered by chance, in a cave at Qumran, by a Bedouin shepherd who was looking for a sheep that had gone astray. All told, seven parchment scrolls, hidden in clay vessels, were discovered in the area. The scrolls are the oldest written extracts of the Scriptures and contain thousands of excerpts of different books of the Bible. Today, some are displayed in the Shrine of the Book at the Israel Museum in Jerusalem.

Mount Masada, in the southern Judean Desert overlooking the Dead Sea, culminates in the impressive site that contains the remains of the Masada fortress. Aerial photographs clearly show the special trapezoid shape of the hill with remains of buildings from the time of King Herod, a water collection system, and the Roman siege system. The natural properties of the isolated cliff, which rises to 1312 ft (400 m), made it an excellent position for a stronghold.

In the early 19th century explorers reached Masada and discovered the fortress. Since then, numerous excavations have taken place that have unearthed most of the constructed area, and restoration and preservation work is still going on. Walls and towers surround the fortress. On the western side archaeologist discovered a large palace with four wings, with three other small palaces located nearby. Visitors can reach the summit by cable car, or on foot along either of two pathways. Masada is one of the most popular tourist sites in the country and attracts large numbers of people. In 2001 UNESCO designated the Masada complex as a World Heritage Site.

The Dust of Time

Caesarea is situated on the Mediterranean coast and incorporates a national park, archaeological sites, a theater and a beach. One can see the remains of the ancient city that served as the capital in the Roman-Byzantine era. In 25-13 BCE Herod built a magnificent port there; it was the largest Mediterranean port at the time. A 9.3-mile (15-km) supply system was built to provide the city with water, incorporating tunnels and an aqueduct supported by arches.

From the air one can see the impressive aqueduct running along the coastline; it is one of the most impressive construction and development projects of ancient times. The first antiquities survey was conducted at Caesarea in 1873 and in 1945 the first excavations began under the auspices of the Mandatory government. Since then, excavations have been in progress almost continually, incorporating the ancient Herodian port, which is most parts have sunk into the sea, and the theater which has a seat-ing capacity of almost 4000 – where concerts are still held.

The Tzipori National Park is located in the center of the Galilee area and contains remains of the ancient city of the same name. Tzipori was known as a beautiful city; in fact, Josephus called it "the ornament of all Galilee." The main sites there include a Roman theater on a hillside, from where one can view Beit Natufa Valley. On the top of the hill there is a Crusader fortress, a residential buildings from the early 3rd century CE, with an impressive mosaic, "the Mona Lisa of the Galilee," an ancient synagogue, houses and an aqueduct. Excavation work there is still in progress.

From the end of the 1960s much of the excavation work in the country has been devoted to Jerusalem. There is an excavation site at the foot of the southern wall of the Temple Mount, with an archaeological park – the Davidson Center – in addition to the Western Wall. There are other sites in the Jewish Quarter and the City of

FLYING HIGH ISRAEL

The Tel Beersheba National Park is located to the east of the city of Beersheba. One of the most sophisticated finds discovered there is an advanced water collection plant that incorporates a 49-ft (15-m) square shaft connected to a large reservoir that collects floodwater.

David, and all relate the fascinating tale of the city. The excavations unearthed many finds from different eras, particularly from the times of the First and Second Temples.

In 1986 a 1st-century BCE fishing boat was discovered in the Sea of Galilee, and in 1985 a 2500-year-old Phoenician ship was found near the Maagan Michael shore. The ship was found in its entirety, with ropes, an anchor, pottery vessels and equipment. It was drawn out of the sea in a technologically advanced project that still arouses great interest. The ship was preserved and is displayed at the Maritime Museum in Haifa.

In the northern Negev lie the remains of the Nabatean city of Shivta, founded at the end of the 1st century CE, and based on agricultural endeavors. Archaeological excavations there have uncovered a water-collection pool, houses, churches, including baptisteries, and a small mosque which was built in the early Arab Era. Aerial photographs clearly show the remains of the isolated desert settlement. Nearby one can see the remains of terraces and rainwater drainage channels dating from the Byzantine Era.

Israel has an abundance of sites and finds from ancient times. Some have already been excavated, some are currently being excavated, while others wait to be unearthed before they reveal to us some more indications of what life was like here in the past. In contrast with photographs taken of the sites from the ground, aerial photographs provide us with a different angle and dimensions of the sites within their given geographical location (and not as a detached entity) and show us the juxtaposition of the different buildings.

154-155
Caesarea is a port town on the Mediterranean coast which was established in the middle of the 3rd century BCE. Today Caesarea is a national park that contains many archeological finds from different eras. Mount Carmel can be seen in the background.

156
The ancient harbor of Caesarea was built by Herod and became one of the most important ports in the Land of Israel. Nearby Herod built a breakwater which protected the ships anchoring in the port.

157
The Crusader wall of Caesarea, with its turrets, was almost completely destroyed. The remains of the wall are situated near the sea. The wall includes 16 towers and two giant gates.

158

The ancient theater built by Herod had a capacity of 4000. Shows are still put on there.

159

Herod's Palace is built on two levels and juts out into the sea. Geometrically de-signed mosaic floors were discovered there. The 30,000-seater hippodrome, built on the shoreline, can be seen in the background.

160
The aqueduct, with arch supports, is one of the trademark symbols of ancient Caesarea. The aqueduct follows the shoreline.

161
The remains of Caesarea include buildings from different eras, including public buildings, statues, storehouses, market buildings and magnificent residences, and bathhouses with mosaic floors.

FLYING HIGH ISRAEL

163
About 8 miles (13 km) south of Haifa lies the Atlit Crusader fortress, also known as Château Pèlerin.

164-165
Nazareth is located in the Lower Galilee on a ridge of the Nazareth Hills. The modern city is on a slope of the hill facing the old city. Nazareth is the largest Arab city in Israel. Mount Tabor can be seen in the background.

166-167

Nazareth is one of the holiest places in the Christian world. The Church of Annunciation was built in 1969 on the site of the home of Mary, Jesus' mother.

168 and 169

The Tel Megiddo National Park rises to a height of 196 ft (60 m) above the surrounding valley at a junction that leads to Haifa Bay, Akko and Bet She'an. The Tel Megiddo National Park was the site of an early Canaanite city. The archeological site includes the Ivory Palace, other palaces, the gates of the city, stables from the time of King Ahab and the most impressive site is the water system, which contains a 82-ft (25-m) shaft.

170
The Church of the Transfiguration of Christ is located at the top of Mount Tabor.

171
Mount Tabor located in the south of the
Lower Galilee region, near to the Jezreel
Valley – the road winds up to the summit.

172

Remains of the ancient city of Beit Tzeida, from the first century BCE, which were discovered on a 82-ft (25-m) high tel overlooking the Sea of Galilee to the north east of the lake.

173

The Akab Ruins is a Jewish estate house from the Second Temple era which was discovered in excavations at Ramat Hanadiv south of Zikhron Yaakov.

174

The settlement of Corazim is located about 2.4 miles (4 km) north of Capernaum. The site contains a settlement from the early first century CE with a synagogue, ritual bathhouse and cisterns, an oil press and residences.

175 left

Tel Lakhish in the Judean Plains is an important site from the Neolithic Era. Archeological work there unearthed remains of a wall towers, and gates.

175 right

More than 42,000 basalt stones form the ancient stone circle "Rujm al-Hiri," in the Golan Heights.

176 left
Tel Jezreel, in the center of the Jezreel Valley, rises 230 ft (70 m) above the valley.

176 right
Sussita is a Greek-Roman city located at the top of a cliff on the Golan Heights. Archeological excavations are still in progress there.

177
The Tel Hatzor National Park in the south of the Huleh Valley. Numerous historic strata have been discovered here over the years and excavations are still going on there today. The finds include palaces, cult sites, walls, gates and a water system.

178-179

Domus Galilaeae International is a church and priest training center on the Mount of Beatitudes overlooking the Sea of Galilee. The cornerstone was laid here in 1999 and construction was completed in 2005. The building is notable for its modern design that contrasts with the other religious buildings there. The Pope gave an address here on his visit to Israel in 2000.

180

180

Tabgha is one of the places of the Holy Trinity at the northern end of the Sea of Galilee which commemorate the works of Jesus in the region. It was here that the miracle of the loaves and the fish mentioned in the New Testament took place. Tabgha is also known as Heptapegon ("the seven springs") because of the seven springs issued forth here. Today there are only five springs there.

181

Pilger House at Tabgha is a guest house for pilgrims that was built in 1889 around a small church. The historic building was renovated and enlarged, and reopened in 2001.

182
Kursi is an archeological site where remains of a 5th century CE monastery and church were found.

183
The Kursi National Park is situated near to the Sea of Galilee. In the center of the park is a wooden sculpture which has become known for its "special powers." Visitors sit on the sculpture and make wishes.

184
The site at Capernaum where a magnificent ancient synagogue from the 4th century was discovered, with an octagonal church from the 5th century found alongside, which was identified at the house of Peter.

185
The beautiful church on the Mount of Beatitudes, which was built in 1936 by Italian architect Antonio Barluzzi, is designed in an octagonal shape symbolizing the eight verses from the Sermon on the Mount which Jesus gave there.

186
A small complex of red-tiled buildings (left) surrounds the Church of the Multiplication of Loaves and Fishes at Tabgha, by the Sea of Galilee.

187 left
A small basalt church consecrated to St. Peter marks the site where Jesus, after the resurrection, offered a meal to his disciples.

187 right
The Orthodox Greek church of the Seven Apostles. at Capernaum can be seen from a distance due to its red domes and white walls.

188
In a purpose-built facility on the banks of the Jordan River, white-robed faithfuls prepare themselves for the baptism.

189
The cloudy sky is reflected in the fish pools of the Beit She'an Valley. A flock of cormorants hunt for food.

190

The Star of the Jordan Crusader fortress, built in 1140, is located at the edge of the Lower Galilee region. The fortress is made of basalt and surrounded by a wall.

192-193

Beit She'an in the Beit She'an Valley that leads to the north. The National Park contains Tel Beit She'an which rises up 164 ft (50 m) above the surrounding area and which offers a view of the valley and the city of Scythopolis below.

194

194

The magnificent Street of Pillars from the Byzantine Era led from the theater to the foot of the tel in Beit She'an. The street was about 590 ft (80 m) in length and about 24.6 ft (7.5 m) wide.

195
The Roman theater is the most impressive remnant find in Beit She'an, with the magnificent Street of Pillars leading off from it.

196-197
Qumran is located on the north-western shore of the Dead Sea, near the Qumran River estuary. The Dead Sea Scrolls were discovered in caves her. Following their discovery archeological excavations took place here which unearthed the remains of a settlement dating to 150 BCE.

198 and 199
Herodion – a fascinating archeological site from the time of the Second
Temple – contains a fortress and palace built by King Herod.

200-201
Jericho, one of the oldest cities in the world lies about 6.2 miles (10 km)
north of the Dead Sea. There is an abundance of archeological remains
in the city, one the most impressive being the Hisham Palace which was
built in the 8th century as a winter palace.

202 and 203
Masada served as a fortress and one can discern its natural defense advantages – an isolated outcrop which provides a perfect defensive vantage point.

204 and 205
The Masada Cliffs located on the eastern fringes of the Judean desert.
The head of the cliff is a trapezium-shaped plateau surrounded by a
fortified wall 0.86 miles (1.4 km) long with a large number of towers.

206
The most impressive spot on the Masada hilltop is the Northern Palace built by Herod. There are three steps built in to the hillside. Herod built an enormous bath-house at the summit and 29 spacious storehouses where hundreds of pottery vessels, were discovered.

207
The upper level of the Northern Palace at Masada contains four bedroom. A sophisticatedly designed staircase, built by Herod, leads down to the lower levels.

208
The Northern Palace at Masada is built on three levels. There is a large hall on the middle level, which is surrounded by pillars, and on the lower level. Nearby one can see a small private bathhouse used by the palace residents.

209
The Visitors Center, museum and hostel at the foot of Masada.

210
Ovdat became the major city along the Nabatean trade route between Petra and the port of Gaza. The center of city is located on a hilltop that rises 2132 ft (650 m) above sea level.

211
The impressive sites discovered at Ovdat include residential quarters, an observation tower, a wine press, and remains of churches and a bathhouse.

212-213

The remains of the isolated Nabatean city of Shivta lie scattered in the Negev Desert. In the Byzanthine era, the city was used as a pilgrim's rest place on the road to Egypt and Mount Sinai.

214
Shivta was settled by a Christian community and the remains of three
churches were discovered there. A mosque from the times of the Arab occupation was also unearthed there.

215
Shivta was not fortified and was not situated along any trade routes. As
a result, researchers believe Shivta was an agricultural settlement,

216

216 and 217

The Nabatean city of Mamshit is the smallest of the Negev cities and covers an area of 40 dunams (approx. 10 acres/4 hectares). Archeological excavations there unearthed complete streets with auditoria, courtyards and balconies. Two impressive churches were also found there. Mamshit contains uniquely designed buildings that are not found on any other Nabatean site.

FLYING HIGH ISRAEL

219
Tel Arad was one of the largest cities in Israel. The city is divided into two parts: the lower city which surrounded by a wall, and the more distant raised fortress tel.

THE EASTERN WATER ROUTE FROM THE GOLAN HEIGHTS TO EILAT

FLYING HIGH

FLYING HIGH ISRAEL

221
Land of the Dates – the area of the Jordan Valley contains
numerous palm groves (left). The northern beach of Eilat is an
area of hotels and a marina (right).

The Great African Rift Valley is a chain of geological rifts which impact on Israel, from Mount Hermon in the north to the Gulf of Eilat in the south. The Rift Valley began forming about 25 million years ago and it continues to evolve to this day, stretching from southern Turkey to Mozambique in Africa. In Israel, the Rift Valley traverses the country, from Mount Hermon, which the rift pushed up, along the Jordan River, Kinneret Valley, Dead Sea Valley to the Gulf of Eilat and the Red Sea. Israel is a heavily constructed country and contains many contrasting landscapes in such a small area. One of the contributory factors is the Rift Valley which produced intriguing "topographical shocks," such as the Dead Sea in the middle of the desert.

Interestingly, the bodies of water that formed over the years along the Rift Valley are different from each other, in shape, depth and the type of water they contain.

The Jordan River traverses the length of Israel, along the Rift Valley, and divides the country into two sections: the western side and the eastern side. Three sources of the River flow down the foothills of Mount Hermon – the Dan, Banias and Hatzbani rivers flow into the Sea of Galilee. From above we can view the meandering path of the hilly section of the Jordan, and catch a glimpse of the rafting craft speeding towards the Sea of Galilee. To the northeast of the lake, in the Beit Tzida delta, the rivers merge and form lagoons with rich vegetation and an abundance of water fowl, birds and other wildlife.

The Sea of Galilee is Israel's most important reservoir and, in a rainy year, provides around one third of the country's water requirements. It is the

222
Extensive salt ponds in the Dead Sea Basin create different
shapes and "drawings" on the ground.

The Eastern Water Route
From the Golan Heights to Eilat

starting point of the National Water Pipeline (the country's leading water facility) which channels water from the rainy north to the drier central and southern regions. The pipeline stretches for about 80 miles (130 km), in both closed pipelines and open aqueducts. In the Beit Natufa Valley of the Lower Galilee region we can see a "water artery" heading south.

The Sea of Galilee also serves as a major tourist attraction. Its beaches are well tended and attract large numbers of bathers who also take part in water sports. The main type of tourism in the region features pilgrims who go there to visit the Christian holy places. To the northwest of the lake there is the "holy triangle" area which comprises three churches – Tabgha, the Mount of Beatitudes and Capernaum, which commemorate Jesus' deeds in the area.

Capernaum – an ancient fishing village where, besides the remains of a large magnificent synagogue, a Greek orthodox church was built in the 1920s. The church has a Balkan appearance, with round red domes. The church is dedicated to the twelve disciples whom Jesus chose to disseminate his teachings. Higher up, the Mount of Beatitudes church looks down across the entire area and conveys a sense of rich pastoral beauty. According to tradition, the church at Tabitha is where Jesus performed the miracle of the loaves and fishes, which enabled him to feed thousands of his followers.

On the western shores of the Sea of Galilee lies the city of Tiberias which, along with Jerusalem, Safed and Hebron, is considered one of the four holy cities where most of the Jewish population of the Land of Israel (pre-state Palestine) lived. Tiberias's economy is mainly based on regional tourism and offers visitors an abundance of restaurants, hotels and attractions.

Tiberias is built on three levels. The lowest level lies along the shores of the Sea of Galilee and includes the old city, hotels and remains of the Roman-Byzantine city. The middle level lies on the slope of the surrounding hills and is largely occupied by a residential area. The top level is the

The Eastern Water Route
From the Golan Heights to Eilat

newest part of the city, and construction is still in progress there.

The river flows southward from the lake along the Jordan Valley as far as the Dead Sea, for which it is the main source of water. The Dead Sea is a world-renowned natural phenomenon and geological wonder. It is the lowest land-based spot in the world – 1368 ft (417 m) below sea level – and has a very high salt content, which reaches about 30 percent salinity, as well natural resources and materials that are in demand around the world. It is located on the fringes of the Judean desert with the western shore under Israeli control, and the eastern shore under Jordanian control. The high concentration of salts and minerals allows bathers to effortlessly float on the water.

The Dead Sea is also known for its therapeutic qualities and many visitors go there to smear themselves with the mineral-rich mud and to float on the water. In contrast with the blue water of the Sea of Galilee the Dead Sea is green, and sometimes takes on a turquoise shade.

The western section of the Dead Sea features the most visually prominent area, Matzor HaHe'etekim, formed by the abundant geological activity in the region. Most of the streams of the Judean Desert flow here and this led to the formation of dolomite rock caves which, in the past, were used for habitation. The whole of the southern region is breathtakingly beautiful and contains remains of lagoons and silt fans and a wide variety of geological forms; they give the area a striking and unparalleled appearance. Despite the area's aridity, and paucity of water sources, numerous animals live there such as ibexes and desert deer, and rich vegetation flourishes.

In addition to its successful tourism activities, the region also has a well developed quarrying industry. The Dead Sea Works, located to the south, are the world's largest producers of potash and bromide. The salt production plant operates evaporation pools, arranged in straight lines in the Dead Sea's southern basin. From above, the pools look like a table of colors in shades of brown-turquoise-green.

The Eastern Water Route
From the Golan Heights to Eilat

They pools contain the raw materials from which potassium is ultimately produced.

In recent years, swallow holes have appeared on the shore, both as a result of natural evaporation but also as a result of the Dead Sea Works' evaporation pools that are located there. South of the Dead Sea, to the east along the Jordanian border, stretches a long narrow valley known as the Arava.

The Arava is an arid region whose inhabitants earn their living from greenhouse agriculture. A large part of the produce from here is exported. Israeli agriculture is well developed and is based on the most advanced growing methods and one of the best irrigation methods in the world, which produces enormous savings in water. Most irrigation is provided by a drip system. In addition to supplying the national market, Israel is also a major exporter of citrus fruit, fish, chicks, honey, wine and flowers. As a result of this use of the arid Arava region, its unique appearance is enhanced by shades of brown with strips of color provided by the greenhouses and their crops.

Eilat is the Israel's southernmost town, and has a port and airport. Since it was founded in 1951, Eilat has grown from a small fishing village to a prosperous port and tourist resort. It location is uniquely favorable, and far from the heavily populated central region. Most of the hotels and tourist attractions are located along the town's northern seashore.

In Biblical tales, the Red Sea symbolizes the redemption of the Children of Israel as they fled from Egypt. The Book of Exodus, chapter 14 verse 16, says: "Lift up your rod, and stretch out your hand over the sea, and divide it: and the Children of Israel shall go on dry ground through the midst of the sea." The sea split into two and the Children of Israel passed through it. The sea's blue waters do not divulge the story but draw people to them.

The Red Sea is a major tourist attraction. Many visitors go there to bathe and also to dive in the seas and enjoy the rich coral reef and the colorful submarine life. Those who want to enjoy the underwater treasures, but stay dry, can do so at the un-

The Eastern Water Route
From the Golan Heights to Eilat

derwater observatory, which also offers guidance on how to observe this enchanted world. Tourists may also visit the dolphin reef and experience swimming together with these wonderful mammals. The comfortable weather, particularly in the winter, attracts many tourists – especially from Europe – who go to enjoy the sea and sunbathe on its beaches.

Eilat is located at the meeting point of three countries – Israel, Egypt and Jordan – and has two international borders and two border crossing points. The Taba crossing has been open since 1982, following the peace treaty with Egypt, and the border with Jordan was opened in 1994, after Israel and Jordan signed a peace treaty. Another source of income is provided by the seaport and airport, the latter handling both domestic and international flights.

Sandwiched between the Red Sea and the mountains and desert, Eilat enjoys a wonderful location that provides us with a truly colorful view: the city nestles between the brown-red hills, with its white houses descending to the blue waters of the sea. Visitors can take part in hikes and tours, and take a trip to Timna Park, situated about 19 miles (30 km) north of Eilat. Most of the horseshoe-shaped valley is a nature reserve that contains many geological features, and rare and breathtakingly beautiful landscapes and natural elements. The reserve contains a manmade lake with sailing facilities, and copper mines that survive from the mining activity that took place here thousands of years ago.

Other striking features of the park include "the mushroom," which rises up 13 ft (4 m), and Solomon's Pillars at the edge of Mount Timna. The pillars were formed as a result of natural wear and tear that produced cracks in the sandstone. Over the centuries rainwater penetrated and deepened them. Nearby are two sandstone arches also formed through natural wear and tear.

The wildlife near Kibbutz Yotvata is also well worth a visit, where attempts have been made to restore animals – which lived in the region in ancient times – to nature.

228
Mevo Hammah is the southernmost settlement on the Golan Heights at the head of the HaOn Cliffs that drop down to the Sea of Galilee.

229
Hammat Geder, in the south of the Golan Heights, contains healing and leisure pools. The site has five hot springs rich with minerals.

230

Remains of the Nimrod Fortress known as "Nimrod's Braid," which dates from the Middle Ages, is situated at the foot of Mount Hermon.

231

Gamla gets its name from its camel-hump shape (camel = *gamal* in Hebrew). The site is situated in the center of the Golan Heights and contains a nature reserve and archaeological excavations.

232-233
Cereal crops growing on a plateau in the southern Golan Heights near Kibbutz Mevo Hammah.

234
The fields of Kibbutz Kfar Haruv in the southern Golan Heights and the Mitzpeh Hashalom vacation village provide a vantage point of the Kinarot Valley and the Galilee.

235 left
The eucalyptus trees encircle the Yardenit baptism site on the Jordan River.

235 right
The Arbel Cliff rises above the Sea of Galilee and changes hues with the seasons. In summer it is bathed in shades of brown, turning verdant with an abundance of vegetation in the winter.

236 and 237
The hilly section of the Jordan River that stretches for 7.45 miles (12 km) flows down steep slopes and meanders through rocks. In the winter and spring the area is particularly attractive because of the abundance of water and rich vegetation.

238

238
The Jordan Rivers meanders down the hilly area north of the Sea of Galilee.

239
The security area where the Jordan River enters the Sea of Galilee.

240
Kibbutz Alumot is built on a hilltop overlooking the Sea of Galilee and the Jordan Valley.

241
Houses and sunshades on the beach at the Ein Gev vacation village next to the kibbutz.

242 left
Degania, "the Mother of the Settlements", was founded in 1910 and provided a basis for hundreds of kibbutzim that were established after it, and based on a communal lifestyle.

242 right
Kibbutz Ginosar lies on the shore of the Sea of Galilee and engages in fishing, agriculture and tourism.

243
The Jordan River flows out of the Sea of Galilee next to Kibbutz Degania.

244
The city of Tiberias sits along the Sea of Galilee (also known as Sea of Tiberias or Genezareth).

245
Water sports are well developed at the Sea of Galilee, and the local tourist sector is highly prosperous with large numbers of lakefront hotels in Tiberias.

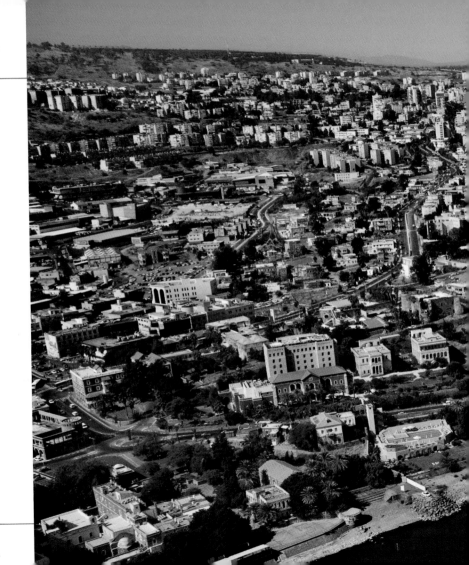

246-247
Tiberias lies on the western
shores of the Sea of Galilee. In the
19th century it was considered
one of the holy cities, along with
Jerusalem, Safed and Hebron,
where most Jews of the time lived.
Today, Tiberias is a resort town
with dozens of hotels.

248

Ramat Yissakhar, which mainly contains agricultural areas with corn and wheat, slopes down to the Yavniel Valley and the Sea of Galilee.

249

The Yavniel Valley facing to the north. The summit of Mount Hermon pierces the clouds. In the summer, the peak is brown and in the winter it is covered in snow and can be seen from afar.

250

The Arik Bridge lies near the Jordan River estuary that flows into the Sea of Galilee. The bridge is named after Arik Shemer, a paratroop officer killed in the area.

251

The Jordan Rivers meanders along its southern exit from the Sea of Galilee next to Kibbutz Degania.

252
Mount Yavniel provides a view of the Yavniel Valley, the Jordan Valley and the Sea of Galilee. The Edom Mountains lie in the distance.

253
Hydro-agricultural development create geometric patterns in the Jordan Valley. The water from the Jordan River is almost entirely used for human purposes.

254-255
A view of the Jordan Valley and meandering Jordan River and fields that line its banks: the Israeli west bank and the Jordanian bank on the east.

256-257
The Jordan Valley between Beit She'an and the Sea of Galilee.

258
The Jordan Valley north of Beit She'an. The fish pools belong to the settlement of Or.

259
Kibbutz Maoz Haim and Kibbutz Naveh Eitan and the agricultural land which includes hydroagricultural areas in the Beit She'an Valley.

260
Agriculture is carried out on a massive scale in hothouses in the Beit
She'an Valley.

261
Kibbutz Tirat Tzvi, in the Beit She'an Valley, is surrounded by agricultural
grounds and hydroagriculture.

262 and 263
The northern area of the Dead Sea contains palm groves that are pre-
dominant in the region.

264-265
The Einot Tzukim Nature Reserve known as Ein Fashkha in the northern area of the Dead Sea. There are dozens of salt springs there which wend their way along the ground and form canyons en route to the sea. The area attracts numerous species of flora and fauna.

266-267
The flaky yellowish rocks of Hawar HaLashon are located next to the village of Moshav Neot Hakikar in the northern Arava region near the Dead Sea.

268
Marlstone rocks surrounded Moshav Neot Hakikar south of the Dead Sea.

269
The Dead Sea Works quarries a range of minerals, principally potash and bromine.

270-271
Winter crops grow in hothouses at Kikar Sedom to the south of the Dead Sea and in the northern Arava region.

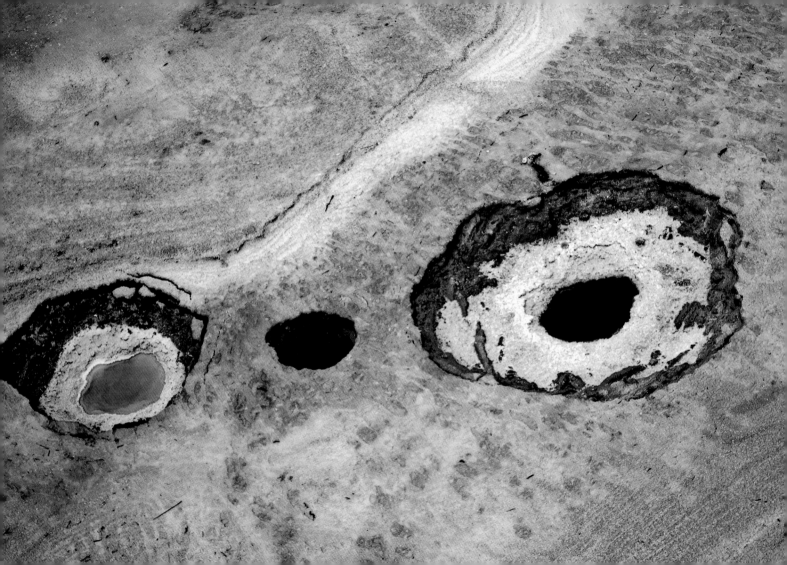

272 and 273
The drop in Dead Sea water level, caused mainly by evaporation, has
created sinkholes of various sizes along its shore, some 131 ft (40 m) in
diameter.

274
The Dead Sea lies along Route 90, which traverses Israel from the Sea of Galilee in the north to Eilat in the south via the Arava region, on the country's eastern border.

275
The salt protrudes above the waterline in the drying pools of the Dead Sea Works.

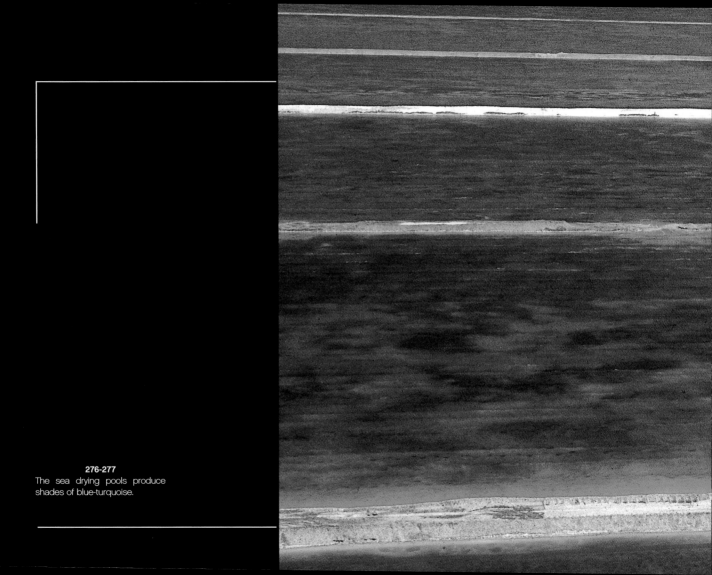

276-277
The sea drying pools produce
shades of blue-turquoise.

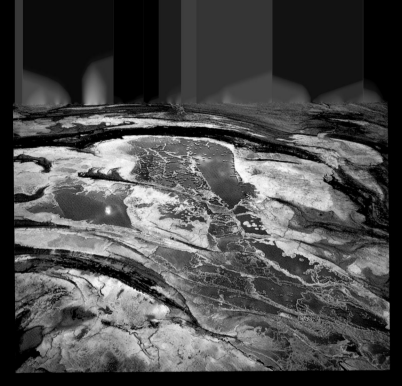

278 and 279

Mineral "drawings" have emerged on the ground in areas where the Dead Sea has receded.

280-281

The minerals create natural "works of art" on the ground where the sea has receded: these are unique to the Dea Sea region.

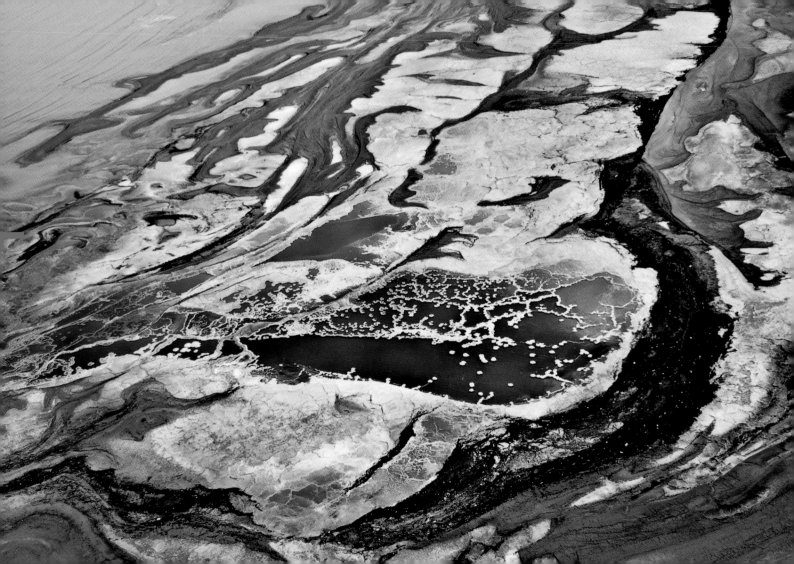

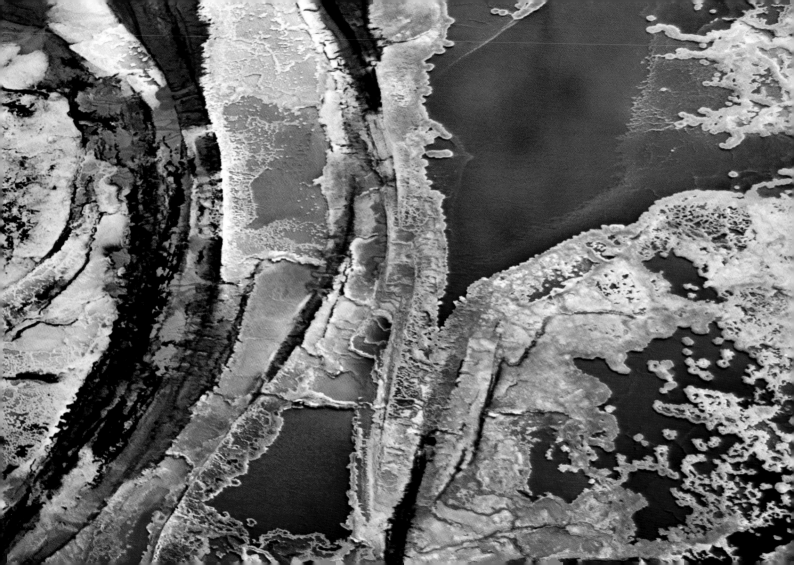

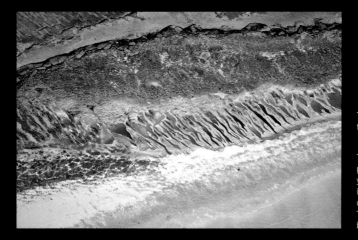

282

The Dead Sea with salt crystals floating on the water.

283

The level of the Dead Sea is dropping by an average of 3.2 ft (1 m) a year. The process of dehydration is worrying and rescue efforts are underway together with Jordan. The recession of the sea creates beautiful textures and sights.

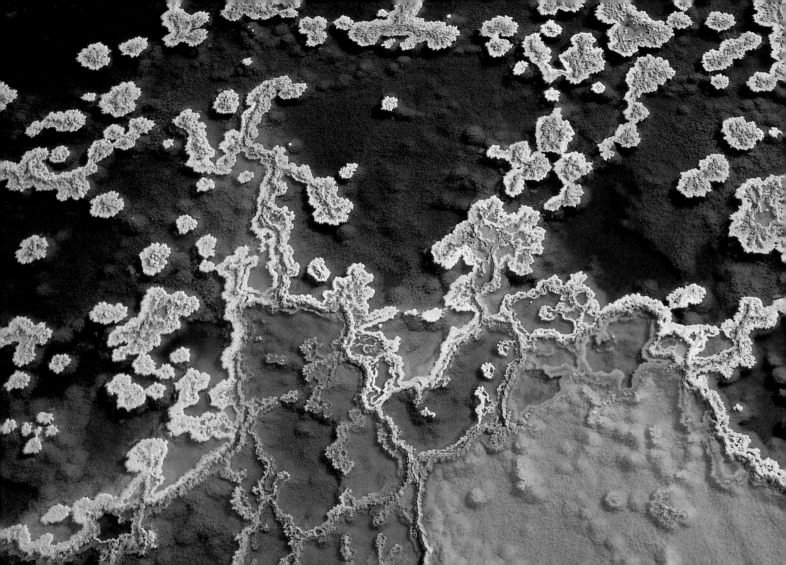

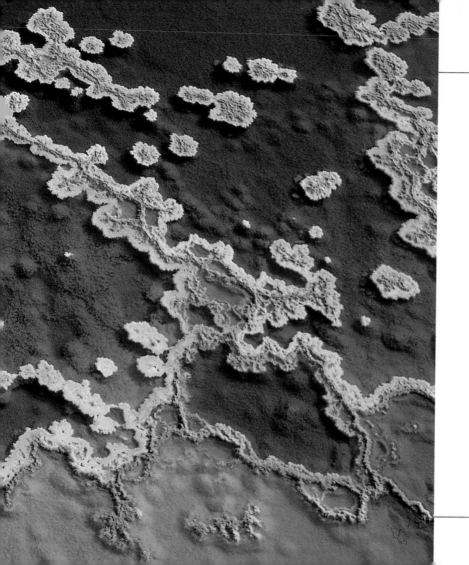

284-285
Salt crystals peep out between the turquoise of the water and create a spectacular abstract show.

286-287
Salt and mineral excavations in the area leave their traces.

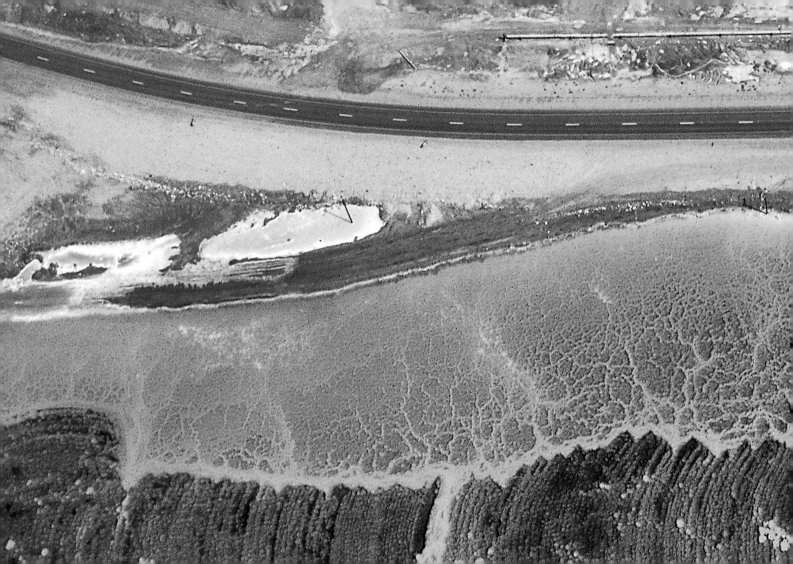

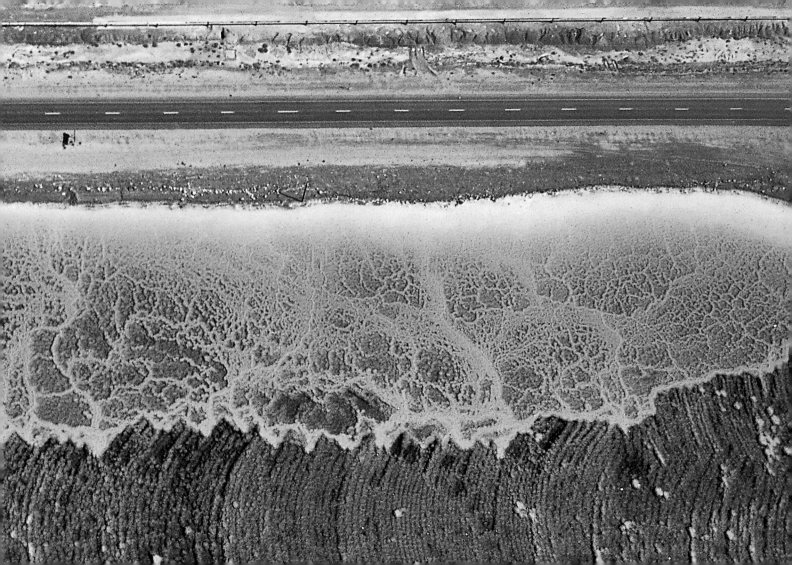

288

288
The Dead Sea offers beautiful beaches for tourists who come to bathe in the waters, for pleasure and for healing purposes.

289
The Dead Sea attracts local and foreign tourism. A view of the hotels at Ein Bokek from the south.

290
The high concentration of salt allows bathers to float effortlessly on the sea.

291
The Dead Sea's therapeutic properties make it a popular tourist site and attract large numbers of bathers.

292
The annual Dead Sea race is run on a 13-mile (21-km) course (half marathon) and takes place in winter.

293
An Israeli flag flies next to a flag of the Philippines with the Dead Sea in the background. The giant flags measure 2165 ft (660 m) by 328 ft (100 m) each. The flags entered the Guinness Book of Records as the largest in the world.

294 and 295
The marlstone rocks, which have undergone a "wrinkling" process offers
a spectacular view of a virginal landscape.

296
The bed of the Arava River contains densely packed rows of agricultural crops which "disturb" the shades of brown and yellow of the tranquil desert.

297
The Dead Sea beach of the land of Ein Gedi is situated near Kibbutz Ein Gedi (in the background).

298
Kibbutz Yotvata in the Arava region shows the typical layout of these labor communities, devoted mainly to agriculture and increasingly to hi-tech industry.

299
The Ein Fashkha nature reserve lies at the north of the Dead Sea and contains salty springs.

300
The Lotz Pits contain 17 ancient water reservoirs on the Ramon ridge. The reservoirs are scattered over an area of about 1.1 sq. miles 3 sq. km) They are hewn out of rock and lined with stones.

301
The Joe Alon Museum, which specializes in Israeli history and Bedouin culture, lies in the Lahav Forest, south of the hills of the Judean Plains.

302
The Tzukim communal settlement in the Arava was established in 1996. The settlement was built on the site of a former army camp.

303
Kibbutz Grofit, in the Arava, was built on a hilltop and provides a view of the southern Arava region and the Edom Mountains.

304 and 305
A view of Eilat surrounded by hills, the hotels and entrance to the marina. Eilat's beaches and hotels are full most of the year.

306 and 307
Two views of the entire bay, Eilat and the city of Aqaba on the other side. The sun shines most of the year in Eilat, and the city is constantly inundated with foreign and Israeli visitors.

308 and 309
The area of the northern beach of Eilat contains most of the hotels and a marina. The beaches contain a promenade and mini-attractions for vacationers.

310
The Coral Beach nature reserve has a bridge that was specially constructed to allow bathers to enter the sea without stepping on the coral
near the shore.

311
The different kinds of sea sports are very popular among local residents
and visitors alike.

312 and 313
Visitors to the Dolphin Reef in Eilat
can swim and dive alongside the
dolphins that swim freely in the sea.

314
The underwater observatory park in Eilat and the Thai vacation village.

315
The underwater observatory park offers visitors an opportunity to meet fish and other marine life without getting wet, and to get a glimpse of underwater life from glass-bottomed boats.

316-317
Eilat – the Princess Hotel and the Taba Hilton Hotel in the distance, on the other side of the Egyptian border.

THE SETTLERS' LAND

Flying High

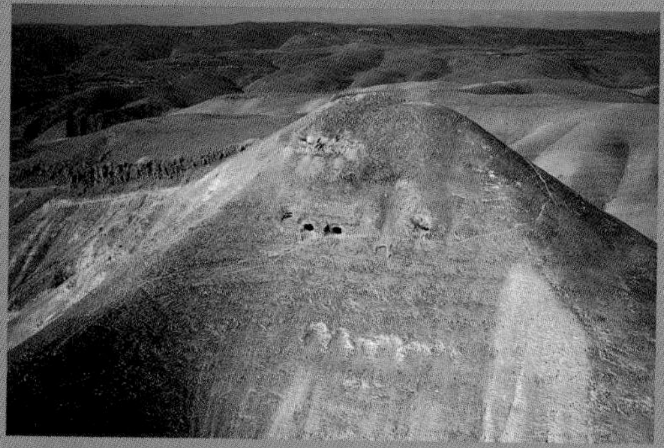
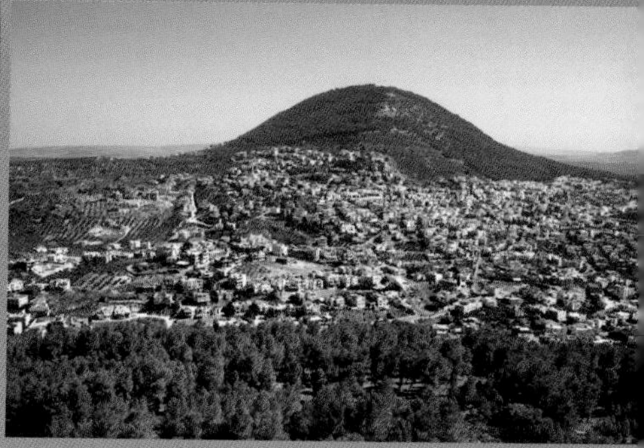

FLYING HIGH ISRAEL

319
Little remains of the Hasmonean fortress on Mount Sartaba, in east Samaria (left).
The village of Kfar Tabor lies at the foot of Mount Tabor in the Lower Galilee, which
rises 1312 ft (400 m) above the surrounding countryside (right).

A bird's-eye view offers the best vantage point for perceiving integration, the melding of natural landscapes and manmade creations.

Millennia and even centuries ago the world looked different. The relationship between mankind and the Earth and Nature was different. Man displayed much respect and honor toward the Earth. He felt it and was aware of it. Man utilized his senses and used the basic and simple materials offered by Nature. Over the years he began to use instruments – for construction and rearranging nature, in a "more convenient manner."

In modern times, the priorities have changed and technological influences have taken over. Construction has accelerated and spread, regardless of natural surroundings; it is focused primarily on creating a more comfortable environment for man in terms of where he chooses to live, and for this purpose he considers such things as proximity to work, educational facilities, etc. In the past, the emphasis on, sense of, and connection to Nature was more dominant. The natural balance was maintained, between the existing resource and manmade creations.

In the area between the Ramon Crater and the Arava a primordial area has survived intact (like the delta area of the Sea of Galilee and parts of the Judean desert). The area is known as "a virgin land" and covers dozens of square miles of wild, natural and virgin desert untouched by human hand.

320
The Zin River forges its way through chalkstone rocks and water holes, known as "marble cisterns," like depressions along the course of the valley where water collects in the winter. The riverbed is about 74 miles (120 km) long and stretches from Mount Ramon in the Arava to the southern area of the Dead Sea.

The Settlers' Land

We are not talking only about natural spots here, but also about urban areas like Tel Aviv which, today, preserves thousands of buildings from the Bauhaus architectural era, which represent a specific era and architectural style. In preserving them we are honoring and appreciating the period, and preserving it for future generations.

At one time, consideration was given to the positioning of structures, from residential buildings to burial structures. The Golan Heights contains evidence of such periods in the form of dolmens which are scattered around the region and look like giant "tables" made of large uncut stones. Researchers attribute them to ancient burial sites, sometimes containing a single burial spot, and sometimes a group funerary site. One special and well-known site, whose special shape can only be viewed from the air, through aerial photography is the Giants' Heap, "Dojem El Hiri" in Arabic. The site comprises over 42,000 basalt stones arranged in open and closed rings. Researchers believe the site dates back between 4000 and 5000 years. The diameter of the outer ring is over 492 ft (150 m), and the whole site stretches out over a plain, with no nearby hills to offer a view of the site. In the past, the site acted as a cult location and some believe the center of it was used for burial purposes.

In 1921, the village of Moshav Nahalal was established in the north of the Jezreel valley. This was a workers' settlement based on principles of equality. Its design and construction followed a circular pattern with the public building placed in the center, accessible to all, around which residential buildings were placed, and with the outer ring used for agricultural purposes. This was a practical design, both in terms of security and with regard to apportioning land, in equal plots (the principle on which the workers' settlement was based) to all 75 families.

In the 1930s and 1940s the kibbutz became the main form of settlement for Jews in Palestine (Eretz Israel). This form of settlement was unique to Israel. The first group, which served as the nucleus for the idea, was established in 1909, at Kibbutz Degania

The Settlers' Land

near the Sea of Galilee. To this day it is known as "the mother of the settlements." The kibbutz society, in its early years, was based on agricultural activities with full equality and partnership in all areas of life. The kibbutz motto was "each according to his needs, and according to his abilities" – based on the principle of equality of human worth. Later, the kibbutzim began to make a living in other areas of production, handicrafts and industry.

An aerial view shows the larger community structures at the center of the kibbutz, including the cultural center, dining hall, main laundry facility, etc. The small red-roofed houses spread out in a circle. Further out are various production facilities, reflecting the kibbutz's areas of activity. The agricultural areas are located in the outer circle, and the kibbutz members access them by vehicle. In contrast with urban living conditions, the kibbutz design incorporates an abundance of gardens and green areas. Pathways wind between the houses and the center of the kibbutz, and roads for vehicles generally run around the outer perimeter, with a small number of inner vehicle access routes.

Over the years, the collective idea receded and kibbutzim have undergone a process of privatization. However, there are still kibbutzim in Israel, and young volunteers still come to work on them from abroad, to get a taste of manual labor and communal life. "Even the stork in the sky knows her seasons. . . ." (Jeremiah, 8, 7)

One of the examples of man's unsuccessful intervention in nature is the Hula Valley. In 1951, a decision was made to drain the marshlands there, in order to prepare agricultural land for the nearby settlements. After the area had been drained it was discovered that the soil was problematic in agricultural terms, and difficult to prepare for growing crops, and a decision was made to refill the spot with water. Today, the Hula Reserve is one of the most beautiful in the country. It looks like a blossoming Garden of Eden and attracts many flora and fauna enthusiasts. Because of the reserve's position, on the migratory

The Settlers' Land

path between Europe and Africa, it acts as an important resting spot for migrating birds. Each year the area hosts over 200 species of birds; they benefit from the waters there. In addition to the birds, the animal life and vegetation are rich, and there are numerous fish and mammals in the reserve.

The situation in Israel has always been complex. The Zionist dream, the declaration of the state, the process of settlement, the land disputes, the juxtaposition of the two nations, with such mixed feelings toward each other, has frequently interfered with growth and progress and led to each side harming the other. The day-to-day security situation was intolerable until, in 2002, the Israeli government decided to establish a separation wall between the Palestinian inhabitants of Judea and Samaria and the Israeli inhabitants.

The wall is the subject of fierce debate between those who support it and those who oppose it. The wall is not yet complete, and no one knows if it ever will be finished. In some areas where the wall has been constructed the number of terrorist attacks has greatly decreased, and almost no suicide bombers have crossed into Israel. On the other hand, one can see from an aerial view that, in some places, Palestinian families have been separated from each other, or homes have been cut off from their land, thereby preventing the families from making a living. Children have to walk for hours to get to school. In practice, the wall separates people from their daily environment and has caused physical and emotional damage. The law-courts are still addressing the matter, and the ultimate route of the wall has yet to be determined. Some parts that were constructed have been demolished by order of the courts, and there is even dispute over terminology – is this is separation wall? A separation fence? Or a security fence?

In the southern Arava, around 18.6 miles (30 km) north of Eilat, lies the Timna Park nature reserve. This is a wide valley with a desert landscape containing large deposits of copper lodes which served as the basis for ancient copper industries in the region.

The Settlers' Land

Here, copper was mined for the first time in history, around 6000 years ago. In geological terms, Timna Park contains an abundance of cliffs of colorful sandstone, in different shapes. Aerial pictures show one of the remarkable spots in the park, the "mushroom," which an impressive rocky outcrop which rises to a height of 13 ft (4 m), made of red sandstone.

The relationship between man and the earth changes daily. There is a growing green trend in the world today, which is also affecting Israel, where organizations are being established to preserve the environment, and to return to nature and its preservation. The green organizations aim to make the world a pleasant place to live in, to educate the public and raise awareness of a range of environmental issues. This also covers supervision and protection of the national parks and nature reserves, land development, planting forests and prevention of environmental damage.

When we look at the map of Israel, which covers an area of only about 8495 sq. miles (22,000 sq. km), we get an idea of its wide range of landscapes. In just one hour one can drive from the hot, humid bustle of Tel Aviv to the peaceful hills of the Judean Desert, with its dry climate. One can leave the green landscapes of the Galilee, with its cool weather and scent of orchards, and head for the hot, brown and arid Arava region. From the Hula Nature Reserve in the north, with its chirping birdlife, one can drive to Jerusalem, which resounds to the sounds of everyday life and the pealing of church bells wafting through the air.

Between the pages of a book, images of Israel combine and merge to form a single complex fabric replete with history, natural components and the deeds of mankind. This a great, impressive and colorful patchwork quilt. "For the Lord God has brought you to the good land, a land of rivers, springs and chasms, gushing forth in valley and in mountain: a land of wheat and barley and vines and dates and pomegranates, a land of olives, oil and honey." (Deuteronomy, 8, 7-8)

326-327
Metulla was founded in 1896 by Baron Rothschild. It is Israel's northernmost town. Metulla lies on a hilly ridge overlooking the Galilee Hills and Mount Hermon.

328

Kerem Maharal is a workers' agricultural settlement (*moshav*) founded in 1949 near Atlit in the center the Carmel Hill region. The *moshav* is named after the legendary 16th century rabbi, the Maharal of Prague.

329

Kibbutz HaGoshrim was founded in 1948 in the Galilee Panhandle. It was given its symbolic name (*gesher* in Hebrew. means "bridge") as it was supposed to serve as a link between Israel and the Diaspora. The Koren riverbed runs along the edge of the kibbutz.

330 and 331
The Emek Habokrim Farm located on the Golan Heights offers horseback treks along the slopes of the hills against a rich green backdrop.

332
Safed, located in the eastern part of the Galilee, is a picturesque town with a comfortable summer climate that attracts many visitors.

333
Amuka is a communal settlement in the north of the country near Hatsor of the Galilee, and Safed. Biria Forest, near the settlement, contains various species of pine trees and covers an area of around 20,000 dunams (approx. 5000 acres/2023 hectares).

334 and 335

In the 16th century, Safed became the spiritual and financial center of the Jewish community in the Land of Israel. Today, one can roam through the narrow and picturesque alleyways of the old Jewish quarter and the nearby artists' quarter. Safed is considered to be "the capital of the Upper Galilee," and is the country's highest city. The city overlooks the Sea of Galilee to the east, and Mount Hermon to the west.

336

Rosh Pina forms part of a group of settlements established during the first wave of Jewish immigrants. The settlement is located on the northeastern slopes of Mount Canaan and overlooks the Golan and the Huleh Valley.

337 left

Moshav Shefer in the center of the verdant area of the Lower Galilee was founded in 1950 on the land of the abandoned Arab village of Faradia.

337 right

Had Ness is a communal settlement in the Golan that engages in tourism and vacation activities.

338-339

Nahalal was the first workers' *moshav* (rural settlement) established in pre-state of Israel Palestine, in 1921, in the northern part of the Jezreel Valley. Nahalal is known for its design and is built like a sun radiating its rays in all directions. The central circle contains the public buildings that serve the entire community, the residential buildings were built in the middle ring, and the outer ring comprises the agricultural plots that are divided equally between the *moshav* members.

340

Kafr Kana is an Arab settlement in the center of the Lower Galilee. There are three churches there: the Franciscan Church of the Wedding where, according to Christian tradition, Jesus turned water into wine at a wedding of poor people, the Greek Orthodox Church of St. George and the Franciscan Church of St. Bartholomew.

341

Kfar Kama in the center of the Lower Galilee is mostly inhabited by Cherkessians from the Caucasus.

342
The Arbel Cliffs rise 1246 ft (380 m) above the Sea of Galilee. The Bedouin
village of Hammam lies next to the foothills, and the settlement of Migdal
can be seen in the far distance.

343
The reservoir at the summit of the Arbel Cliffs overlooks the Sea of Galilee.
There are caves at Arbel where man lived in prehistoric times. Later, the
caves were turned into a large fortress with secret passageways.

344-345
The Yavniel Valley spreads out like a giant patchwork quilt with its agricultural areas, west of the Sea of Galilee in eastern Galilee.

346 and 347
The Jezreel Valley is a large valley between the Lower Galilee Hills to the north and the Samarian Hills to the south. It is the largest continuous cultivated area in the north of Israel.

349
Kibbutz Nir David is located in the northern part of the Beit She'an Valley. The kibbutz sits on the two banks of the Amal River and the Gan HaSheloshah (Sakhneh) National Park is situated in the western part of the kibbutz.

350

The village of Kfar Tabor lies at the foot of the hill. It was founded in 1901 and was originally called "Maskhah," like the nearby Arab village.

351

The bridge that crosses the Akhbara riverbed forms part of the road that bypasses Safed in the north. This is the highest bridge in Israel and its construction (including the construction of the entire road) took, intermittently, twenty years due to opposition from various environmental groups.

352
"A land of wheat, and barley, and vines, and fig trees, and pomegranates;
a land of oil olive, and honey" (Deuteronomy, 8, 8). The Land of Israel was
blessed with seven species of fruit. The olive tree originates from the Middle East and, in Israel, it predominantly grows in the north.

353
Ramat Yissakhar in the aestern Lower Galilee was so called because of
its location in the heart of the part of the Holy Land granted to the tribe
of Yissakhar.

354-355
The precisely "sketched" fruit groves of the Lower Galilee, north of Kfar Tabor.

356
Flat, light brown areas of tilled land contrast with the green patches of rough land left uncultivated by the local farmers in the Northern Negev.

357
An agricultural landscape typical of the olive groves of the Lower Galilee. The stones delineate the plots and prevent rainwater causing soil erosion.

FLYING HIGH ISRAEL

358
Farmers in the hilly regions employ traditional methods of agriculture, including building terraces on the slopes of the hills to form level ground and prevent erosion and loss
of water.

360-361
Most of the area of Samaria is hilly and the ground is difficult to cultivate. That is why terraces were built in order to prevent rainwater from eroding the soil.

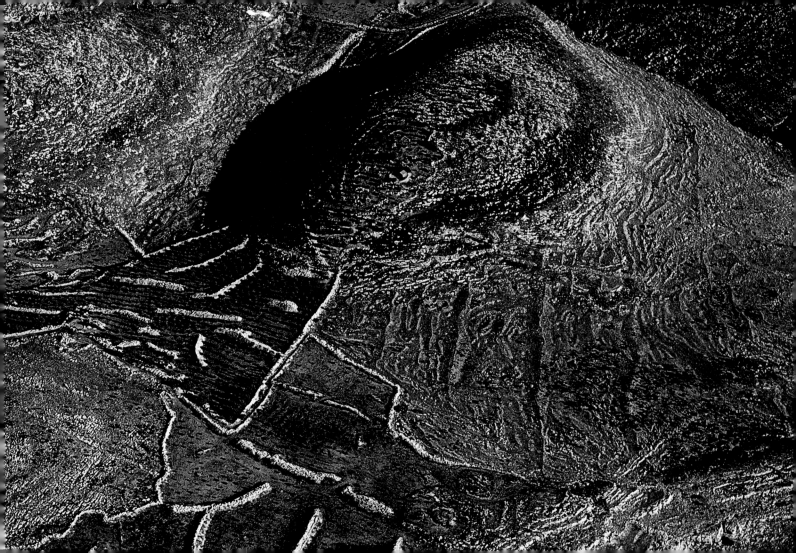

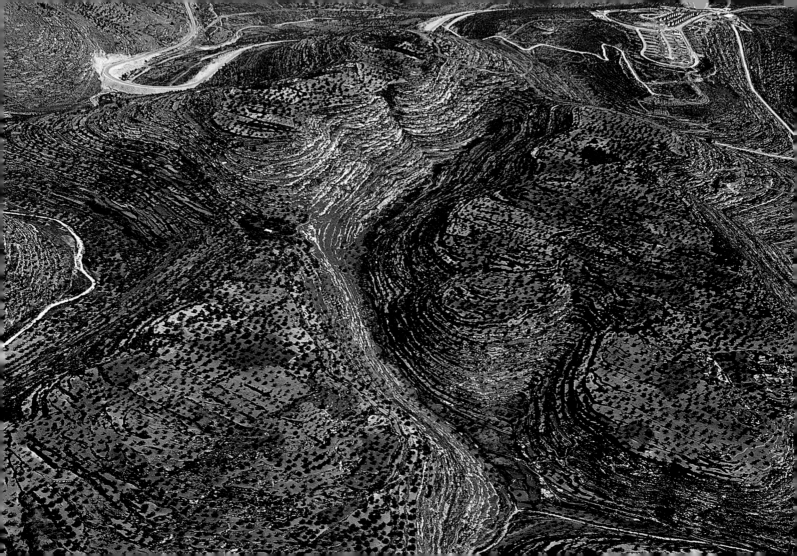

362
The Samarian Hills were formed as the result of a rock movement which
created folds and wrinkles in the rock strata.

363
The Huleh Valley contains natural forests and banana groves.

FLYING HIGH ISRAEL

364
Hothouses with vegetables on the coastal plain. The hothouses are coverer with pro-
tective netting to keep birds out and to filter the sunlight.

366

366-367
"The Shepherds' Fields" 1.2 miles (2 km) east of the Church of Nativity in Bethlehem, is located near Beit Sakhor and contains one of the secret Christian sites. The site is identified with the story of the angel's arrival to tell the shepherds about the birth of Jesus.

368-369
Mount Tabor and the sorrounding area offer stunning views from the sky: the plain and the rolling hills are dotted with odd geometrical patterns, created by settlements and platations.

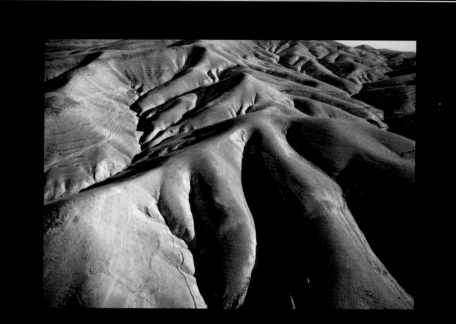

370
Chalkstone hills make up most of the Judean Plateau. The Dead Sea can be seen on the horizon.

371
The beautiful landscape of the Judean Desert with thousands of rounded outcrops interspersed by channels. The area is unchanged by man, and there are no archaeological remains here due to the difficulty of constructing buildings in the region.

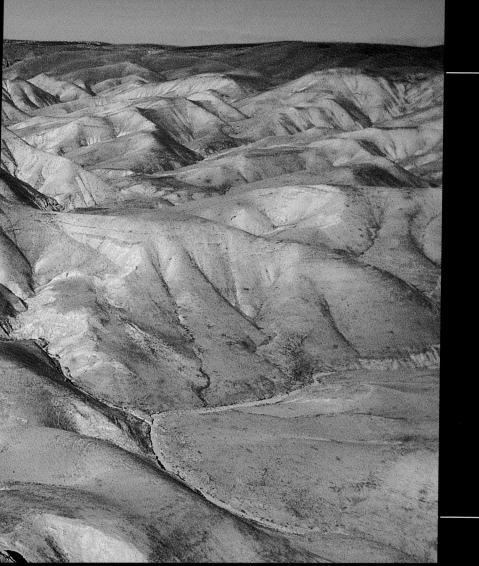

372-373
Though averaging 1312 ft (400 m)
in height on the sea level, the
mountains of Eastern Samaria
near Mount Sartaba rise about
229 ft (700 m) above the valley
floor.

374

The Rahaf River flows into the Dead Sea from the Judean Desert. The lower section of the riverbed cuts through a deep canyon whose walls rise up 492 ft (150 m).

375

The Karnatal is one of the most beautiful monasteries in Israel. It sits on a hillside and overlooks Jericho. The monastery was founded at a time when monks began to live in seclusion in the natural caves of the mountain.

376
The Peratsim Valley is with cracked marlstone rocks. The walls of the riverbed are adorned with "frescoes" created by the fine layers of marlstone rock.

377
The Ein Gedi Nature Reserve in the northern Judean Desert is a beautiful oasis that incorporates the David River valley and the Arugot River valley where water flows all year round. The nature reserve contains abundant vegetation and many animals.

378-379

The Marsaba Monastery is, today, inhabited by some 20 monks who maintain a regimented and highly austere lifestyle. The monastery is not linked to the main water, electricity or telephone networks. Entry to the monastery is limited to men only.

380
Nebi Moussa is a mosque built in a typical medieval classic Islamic style.
The mosque is located in the heart of the Judean Desert.

381
The Greek-Orthodox St. George Monastery, dating from the Byzantine Era,
is built on three levels above the Wadi Kelt valley in the Judean Desert.

382-383
In the northern region of the Arava, a primeval landscape of ravines was
created by the collapse of sedimentary rocks onto HaLashon's Lake floor.

384-385
The camel is known as the "desert ship," due to its build and ability to adapt to the conditions of the desert. There are a number of Bedouin villages along the boundary of the Judean Desert whose inhabitants herd camels along the desert plateau.

386-387

Moshav Lakhish in the Northern Negev has around 4000 dunams (approx. 1000 acres/404 hectares) of vines, of grapes grown for fruit, which provide their main source of income. The *moshav* markets the produce both in Israel and abroad.

388-389

Vineyards near Lakhish display engineered shapes dictated the topography of the region.

390

390-391
The World War Two explosives dumps of the British air force lie scattered over the area, in the Western Negev region west of Kibbutz Be'eri.

392
The Lahav Forest is located on the hills of the southern Shfelah region and provides an island of green covering an area of over 30,000 dunams (approx. 7500 acres/3035 hectares).

393 left
Hummus fields in the southern Shfelah region. Hummus requires a relatively small amount of water and mostly uses rainwater.

393 right
"Wine gladdens the heart of man" (Psalms 104, 16), vineyards in the southern Plains region.

394-395
Pine trees account for most of the Lahav Forest in the southern Shfe-lah region. There is colorful inter-play between the shades and shapes of the green forest and the yellow-brown stripes of the de-nuded plowed fields.

396
The Bakai is a type of 2-seater flying ATV used for pleasure trips, here flying over fields of the Negev.

397
Ultralight aviation is a very popular sport in Israel. Some fly ultralight aircraft on weekends while others use them as their regular mode of transport. The aircraft fly at low altitudes of about 500 ft (152 m) and, other than specific routes, all the area over Israel is open to these aircraft.

398
Trees are planted between the cultivable areas (in places where it is not possible to grow crops) and create a spectacular view of shades of green in the Northern Negev.

399
The tamarisk trees are the only vegetation capable of thriving in the arid conditions of the Negev desert. Their roots stretch down deep into the earth in search of groundwater.

400

"Like clay in the hand of the potter" (Jeremiah 18, 6), agricultural fields in the northern Negev near Kibbutz Dorot. A farmer tills his fields between ravines that create intriguing shapes.

402-403

The "common anemone" is a widespread protected wildflower in Israel. In the winter anemones can be found all over the country, from the northern reaches to the Negev plateau. During the short spring season red carpets of anemone proliferate in the Northern Negev.

FLYING HIGH ISRAEL

405
The agricultural work in the Ruhama ravines in the Northern Negev creates intriguing "drawings."

406
A low-flying airplane casts its shadow over hothouses in the Western Negev.

407
Sdeh Nitzan, in the Eshkol district of the Negev, operates hothouses.

408
The Western Negev incorporates a circular irrigation system that produces circular fields.

409
Moshav Ein HaBesor is located in the Eshkol district of the Western Negev. The *moshav* was established in 1982 by former residents of Yamit who were evacuated following the Israeli withdrawal from the Sinai Peninsula. Most of the residents of the *moshav* engage in agricultural activities, such as the cultivation of flowers, vegetables, spices and fowl.

410
The HaBesor Reservoir in the Western Negev forms part of a chain of reservoirs established to collect water supplied from the HaShapdan water purification plant in the Gush Dan region.

411
A group of pelicans stop to rest near the Mediterranean beaches between Dor Beach and Habonim Beach.

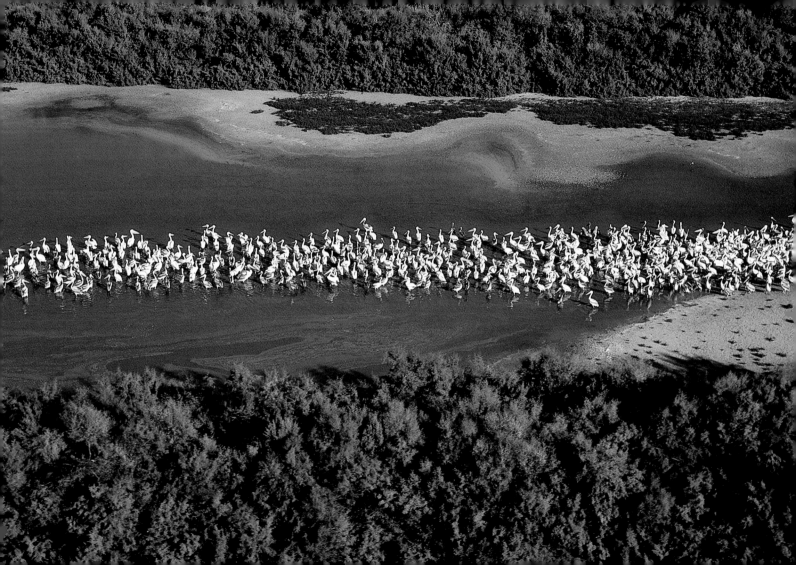

412

The Eshkol National Park, at the foot of a hill, lies in the HaBesor Valley where the waters of the Ein HaBesor spring form warm pools that maintain a temperature of 20 °C (68 °F) all year round.

413

The Eshkol National Park is a green oasis in the Western Negev. The park is a popular nature site covering an area of 3500 dunams (approx. 900 acres/364 hectares).

414 and 415
Extremely rationalized agricultural techniques are necessary on the bare
soils of the Western Negev (here, spinklers irrigate potato fields, right, and
fruit groves, left). From the air, these techinques add a totally unexpected
pattern to the land.

416

The Nitzana River starts at Mount Ramon and stretches along a wide flat valley that contains remains of ancient agricultural activity.

417

"And Isaac departed thence, and pitched his tent in the valley of Gerar, and dwelt there" (Genesis, 26, 17). The Gerar Valley stretches out between Kibbutz Lahav and Kibbutz Re'im, and is the largest tributary of the Besor River. Numerous archeological remains from various eras were discovered along the riverbed, including from the Bronze Age.

418-419
The Gerar Valley cuts through the loess soil and creates a spectacular landscape.

420

420

The Shikma River starts to the south of Mount Hebron and ends at the Mediterranean Sea south of Zikkim. The valley runs along the seam between a region with a Mediterranean climate and an area with a desert climate. The Shikma Reservoir is located about 0.9 miles (1.5 km) before the river estuary. Water is drawn from the reservoir to enrich the groundwater in the south of the coastal plain.

421

Highway 6 is a main transport artery in Israel which offers a rapid freeway route between the north and south of the country. It is about 53.4 miles (86 km) long, and stretches from the Iron Interchange in the north to the Sorek Interchange in the south.

422

Beersheba was the only city founded by the Turks during their 400-year rule of Israel. The only buildings are preserved in the city center, with the new city constructed around them. The mosque is one of the landmark Ottoman buildings there.

423

The engineering academic college in Beersheba, which was established in 1995, is now the largest engineering college in Israel.

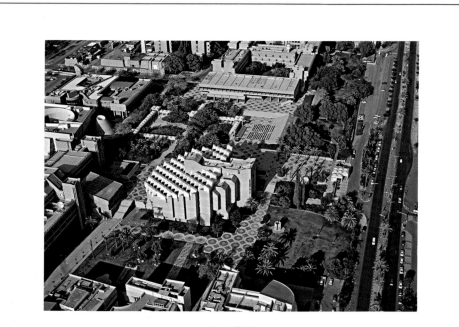

424 and 425
Ben-Gurion University was established in Beersheba in 1969. The picture
on the right shows the University's main library.

426

Sdeh Bokker is located on the northern Negev plateau. The site includes a kibbutz and an academy. The site became famous in 1953 when Israel's first Prime Minister, David Ben-Gurion, moved there with his wife Paula.

427

The Ben-Gurion Academy and the burial site of David Ben-Gurion and his wife Paula overlook the Tzin Valley and it is located near the academy. The country's other leaders are all buried on Mount Herzl in Jerusalem.

428
Located in Timna Park, in the Negev, the Solomon's Pillars (the parallel rock "blades" outlined by shadow in the center of the image) are rock formations produced by natural erosion typical of red chalkstone. The pillars rise to a height of 131 ft (40 m).

429
The Timna Valley lies in the middle of a basin that extends about 24.8 miles (30 km) northward of Eilat. The valley is shaped like a crater surrounded on three sides by 1312-ft (400-m) high cliffs.

430

The Magic Sunrise resort at Kibbutz Eilot, 1.8 miles (3 km) north of Eilat, allows visitors to enjoy the beauty of the desert.

431 left

Northeast of the Ramon Crater, Mount Ardon walls rise 656 ft (200 m) above the base of the crater.

431 right

The Antelope Farm, a sort of African safari site in the Arava, contains various species of animals and provides accommodation and leisure activities.

432-433

The Nekarot River is a riverbed that drains the Ramon Crater.

434

Mount Arif contains two craters which are the smallest of the Negev craters. One is at the top of the hill and the other lies on the western slope. The top of the hill offers a view of Mount Negev, the Edom Mountains and the Arava.

435

Trekkers walking along the top of Mount Arif which rises up several hundred feet above the surrounding area.

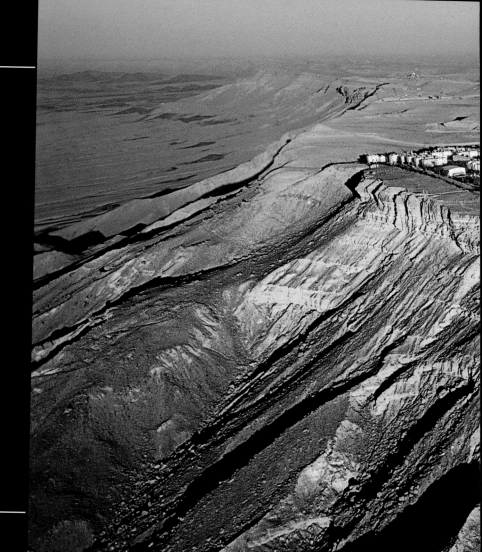

436-437
...tzpeh Ramon is located at the
...ge of the Ramon Crater and
...erlooks it. The town started out
...1951, as a camp for the quarry
...orkers in the crater.

438

Makhtesh Katan is the smallest of the three Negev craters, although it is said to be more beautiful. Almost circular in shape, this erosive valley is about 5 miles (8 km) long and 4.3 miles (7 km) wide.

439 left

The Ramon Crater, formed by the erosion of soft rock strata, is 24.8 miles (40 km) in length and 5.5 miles (9 km) across at its widest part.

439 right

The Visitors' Center, located at the edge of the Ramon Crater cliff, provides information about the natural phenomena of the region.

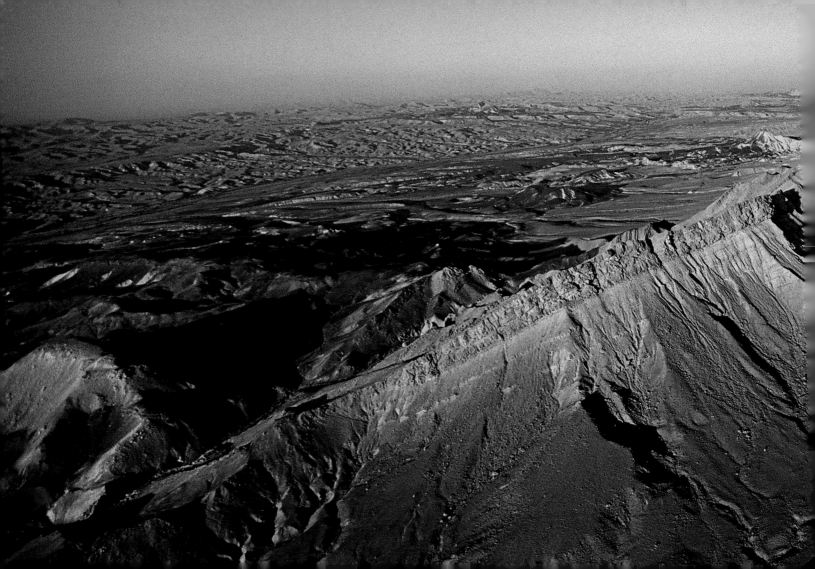

440-441
The southern wall of the Ramon Crater rises up 984 ft (300 m) above the crater floor. The enormity of the crater, and the various rock strata, are clearly visible.

442-443
The small Mitzpeh Ramon, because of the unfavourable position and the relative poverty of the region, is going to fling itself as an agritourist centre.

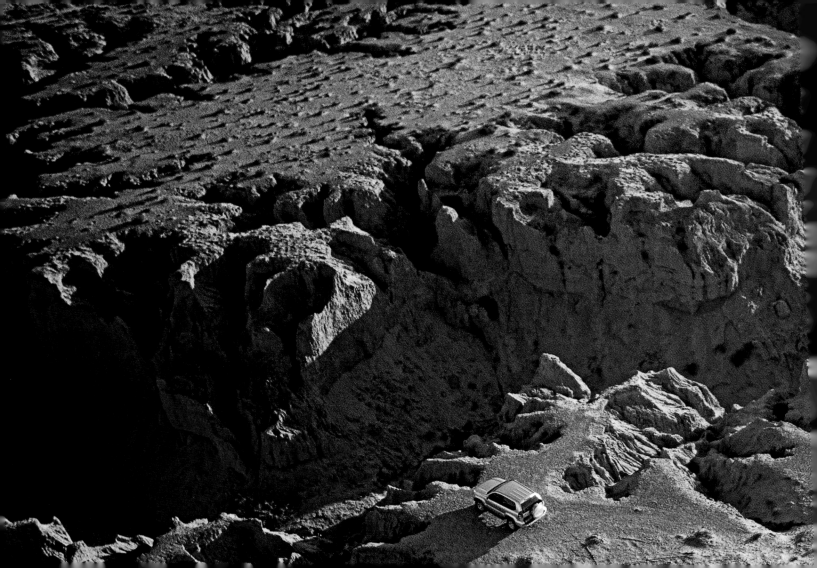

444-445
In Western Negev, a car stops at the edge of the chalkstone cliffs which were pounded by water that cracked the stone and created beautiful shapes.

446
A view of the upper section of the Hawarim riverbed near the Sdeh Bokker Academy. The riverbed cuts through the marlstone rocks and creates a wrinkled rock effect.

447
The steep Hawarim riverbed on the northern Negev plateau cuts through the marlstone rocks.

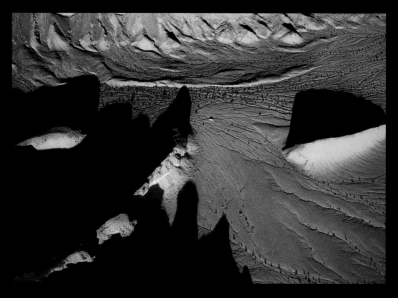

448
Light and shadow "games" appear in the valley of the Ketsara River. The ancient Spice Road, used to transport merchandise from Asia to Europe, follows the river.

449
The Tzin Valley is a wide valley that runs along the boundary of the northern Negev plateau and the Ovdat Heights.

450
The Nafha Plateau in the Negev is covered in a soft blanket of golden brown.

451
The pictures drawn by the wind on the chalkstone rocks are typical of Mount Negev on the Nafha Plateau.

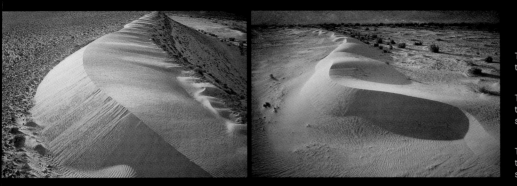

452 left
The texture of the top sands is so fine and soft that the wind sculpts them into different shapes.

452 right
The top sands take on different shapes, like long twisty snakes that take on a golden hue in the sunset.

453
The top sands are formed by the eroded dust of the chalkstone rocks blown by the wind to the slopes at the Ovda Valley's eastern end.

FLYING HIGH ISRAEL

455
Ovda Valley is covered by top sands. The sands are fine, pleasant and delicate. It is fun to walk on them barefoot or to roll about on them.

456
Two spectacular images of hot air balloons floating between the cliffs in the Timna Valley. Noah's Ark was built during the Great Flood but here it "floats" in the arid Timna Valley.

457
Timna Valley, in the southern Arava, is surrounded on three sides by sheer 1312-ft (400-m) high cliffs.

458-459
The Timna Valley, located about 12.4 miles (20 km) north of Eilat in the southern Arava region, contains rare geological forms resulting from past copper mining activities. A hot air balloon event imbued the valley with even more colors.

Index

Index

Index

HANIT ARMONN WAS BORN IN ISRAEL IN 1964 AND STUDIED PARENTAL GUIDANCE AT THE ADLER INSTITUTE. FOR SEVERAL YEARS SHE HAS COMBINED THIS FIELD WITH WORKING ALONGSIDE ITAMAR GRINBERG IN ESTABLISHING AND OVERSEEING PHOTOGRAPHIC ARCHIVES OF PICTURES OF ISRAEL. SHE WORKS CLOSELY WITH ADVERTISING AGENCIES, PUBLISHING HOUSES, ARCHITECTS, MAGAZINES AND PUBLICISTS. SHE CONTRIBUTES TO PHOTOGRAPHIC PRODUCTIONS IN ISRAEL AND AROUND THE WORLD.

Photo credits

All photographs are by Itamar Grinberg except the following:
Marcello Bertinetti/Archivio White Star Pages 12-13, 50-51, 54-55, 61, 63, 358, 370
Itamar Grinberg/Archivio White Star Pages 8 and 9, 18, 34-35, 49, 66, 67 right, 71, 78, 81, 115 right, 128, 131, 141, 144 and 145, 163, 184, 187 left and right, 198 end 199, 200, 228 end 229, 230 end 231, 239, 243, 244 end 245, 251, 252, 275, 276-277, 286-287, 290, 356 end 357 left end right, 375, 405, 439 right
Lior Parag Page 16

With much love to our children Daniel & Keren Grinberg

Dedicated to my parents Rina and Richard for teaching me to explore and to get to know this unique country from the day I was born. - Hanit

The author would like to thank the following people for their help:
Nir Tal, Boaz Peleg, Eitan Kempel - Masada, Ami Marmor, Shilo, Mike, Ravit Naor.

© 2008 WHITE STAR S.p.A.
Via Candido Sassone, 22-24
13100 Vercelli - Italy
WWW.WHITESTAR.IT

Translation from Hebrew to English: Barry Davis

© 2008 STEIMATZKY (2005) LTD
Published simultaneously in Israel by:
STEIMATZKY (2005) LTD
Steimatzky House, 11 Hakishon Street
P.O. Box 10333, Bnei Brak 51114, Israel
Tel: 972-3-5775766
Fax: 972-3-579-4567
email: info@steimatzky.co.il
internet: www.steimatzky.co.il

ISBN 978-965-236-555-2

Reprints: 1 2 3 4 5 6   12 11 10 09 08
Printed in China

464

On a landing strip, opposite
Masada, the largest flag in the
world – an Israeli flag – is spread
out and gains entry into the
Guinness Book of Records. (The
small "cubes" next to the flag are
buses and cars).